DANGEROUS IDEAS

ALF REHN

DANGEROUS IDEAS

WHEN PROVOCATIVE THINKING
BECOMES YOUR MOST VALUABLE ASSET

Marshall Cavendish
Business

This book was first publised in Swedish as *Farliga Idéer* by
BookHouse Editions AB
Riddargatan 17D, S-114 57 Stockholm, Sweden
Copyright © 2010 BookHouse Editions AB

English translation copyright © 2011 Marshall Cavendish International
This English edition published in 2011 by special arrangement with BookHouse Editions AB
by Marshall Cavendish Business
An imprint of Marshall Cavendish International

PO Box 65829
London EC1P 1NY
United Kingdom
info@marshallcavendish.co.uk

and

1 New Industrial Road
Singapore 536196
genrefsales@sg.marshallcavendish.com
www.marshallcavendish.com/genref

Marshall Cavendish is a trademark of Times Publishing Limited

Other Marshall Cavendish offices:
Marshall Cavendish Corporation. 99 White Plains Road, Tarrytown NY 10591–9001, USA
• Marshall Cavendish International (Thailand) Co Ltd. 253 Asoke, 12th Floor, Sukhumvit
21 Road, Klongtoey Nua, Wattana, Bangkok 10110, Thailand • Marshall Cavendish
(Malaysia) Sdn Bhd, Times Subang, Lot 46, Subang Hi-Tech Industrial Park, Batu Tiga,
40000 Shah Alam, Selangor Darul Ehsan, Malaysia

The author and publisher have used their best efforts in preparing this book and disclaim
liability arising directly and indirectly from the use and application of this book.

All reasonable efforts have been made to obtain necessary copyright permissions. Any
omissions or errors are unintentional and will, if brought to the attention of the publisher,
be corrected in future printings.

A CIP record for this book is available from the British Library

ISBN 978-981-4328-04-3

Printed and bound in Great Britain by TJ International

CONTENTS

A WORD OF WARNING

This book won't be as nice and cuddly as books on creativity tend to be. Quite the contrary: it will be a bit angry, and more than a little contrarian, and you may find it uncomfortable and troublesome. In fact, I hope you do. It won't be as helpful and kind as other books – those that promise to make you more creative through sets of fun and happy exercises – and there's nothing accidental about that. The thing is, if you want to become more creative, you have to be challenged, not coddled, and me worrying about whether you're in your happy place or not won't help us one bit. So in stark contrast with many other books in the genre, this one won't mollycoddle you, will say things without mincing words, and will sometimes be downright mean about it. I'll use bad language, be cranky, and you can be damn sure that I won't deliver a lot of motivational cheers. Instead, I'll start from the assumption that creativity is difficult and demanding. I'll assume that in order to summon more creativity you'll have to change the way you look at it and your own thinking processes, and challenge a whole lot of other things – including the notion of creativity itself.

Consider yourself warned.

The author
(Alf Rehn, a man not known for his sunny disposition, and who certainly ain't your mama...)

INTRODUCTION: PROVOCATION AND THINKING DANGEROUSLY

Pure Digital Technologies wasn't what you'd call a huge mover in its industry – quite the contrary. The company was an also-ran, a marginal player that had focused on a disposable video camera. This had been sold in collaboration with a chain of pharmacies, building on the business model of disposable cameras, and had been a modest success in its niche. It was a modest product from a modest company: nothing to be ashamed of, but neither revolutionary nor particularly innovative. Still, the company had bigger plans. One day, they decide to test something new, namely a proper video camera. But there was a problem. Pure Digital Technologies realized they couldn't compete with the major corporations in the market. They did not have the resources to keep up with the competition in product development, and they didn't have the finances to compete on price in the existing segments. Simply put, they couldn't make a better video camera, even if they wanted to.

This is a situation that many companies will recognize. When you're not a market leader, you rarely have the resources to seriously challenge the established players in the field. In the rat race of competition, some will always find themselves left behind when it comes to developing better products. Quite often this leads to apathy, a loser's mindset, decline and death. In such a situation, happy-go-lucky calls for "innovation" or "creativity" really don't seem all that helpful. What is the point of developing a brilliant idea when you know it will be picked up by the competition? Oh, and good ideas are often really, really expensive…. So what did Pure Digital Technologies do?

In hindsight, it was simple, even obvious. Since they couldn't compete by building a better video camera, they simply chose to build a far worse one instead. This might seem like an odd thing to want to do, but it just happened to be genius, a ***truly dangerous idea*** whose time had come. Pure Digital had noticed that older, somewhat less developed methods to capture digital video had become cheap as most companies were obsessing over the newest and best technologies. This led to a situation where you could buy the basic technology for capturing rather grainy video for a pittance. Pure Digital packaged this into a cheap plastic casing, and since they didn't want to spend tons of money on developing fancy functions for it, they didn't. Instead, their product only had the bare essentials – a button for recording, another for playing, one more for erasing and very little else. The only "extra" was an integrated USB port for attaching it directly to a computer. It was small, cheap, insanely simple to use and thus perfect for both the YouTube-generation and people who thought normal video cameras were too complicated, not to mention expensive.

At its release in May 2006, the video camera was called a "Pure Digital Point & Shoot", but this was quickly changed to "Flip Video". In September 2007 the slightly more developed Flip Ultra was released, and immediately became one of the best-selling video cameras in the world. In a few short years, the Flip captured the lion's share of the market, and became the number one product in its segment – 1.5 million Flips were sold globally. And the company? It grew almost 50,000 per cent in five years, and was later acquired by Cisco for $590 million US. Not bad for a marginal player with a technically sub-standard product.

One easily misses the important point of this little story. Too often we focus solely on the company that launched a game-changing product, and forget the most important question: *why didn't the others think of the same thing?* Many, many companies had the opportunity, but didn't make anything of it. And we often forget another thing. The problem is not in the knowledge we have, but in how we imagine utilizing this knowledge. The truth is, the rest of the industry did not look at the Flip and curse itself for not having created it. On the contrary! They thought that the Flip was *disgusting*.

If this strikes you as odd, imagine yourself to be a specialist in video cameras. Your entire working life has been an education in improving and developing them, giving the customer the very best video camera you can make. Suddenly, a company you've never heard of turn up and present something that is far worse than what you're working on, with far fewer functions. Would you be annoyed? Of course you would! This new thing would be in conflict with everything you represent, with everything you believe in. In fact, it would probably feel more than a little threatening. In much the same way that low-cost airline Ryanair managed to annoy the airline industry by removing every vestige of service, and to do so in a sensational fashion, the Flip represented an idea that was seen as dangerous in its context.

We often imagine creativity as something that is pleasant, fun and lovely, and that good ideas are such that everyone smiles encouragingly when confronted with them. But this is a lie and a misunderstanding. On the contrary, real creativity tends to be a little dangerous, threatening, in your face. People in the video camera business tried to be creative and think outside of the box. But as they couldn't handle ideas that were uncomfortable or threatening, the nasty surprise that was the Flip caught them unawares. The Flip was truly a dangerous idea, and the way it made industry people uncomfortable was its greatest triumph.

So, in line with this, the book you're reading won't be one on creativity as it is talked about in workshops. This notion of creativity has become a neutered and diluted concept. Instead, this book deals with *how you can develop dangerous thinking*. Books on creativity tend to be repetitive affairs, going through the same old stories and repeating the same tired sentiments. They tend to be obsequious things, dedicated to feel-good soppiness. This book tries to be a little different. It will confront uncomfortable matters, things that feel as troublesome to us as the Flip must have felt to its competitors. The reason for this is simple: it is when we are forced out of our comfort zone that we can find the radically new, the dangerous, the things that question *the status quo*.

Change is never a comfortable, painless process, and neither is serious creativity. Despite this, creativity is often talked about as though it were a harmless teddy bear, a cute and fuzzy concept that we can all embrace effortlessly. This book wants to annihilate that myth.

Towards More Dangerous Thinking: Five Steps

Those people who challenge the way we act and think – in a business, in an industry or in society – have all been individuals who have found ways to take thinking just that one step further. This is not the same thing as "creativity", not in the limited sense of the word. This is something far more radical. Flip was not just a creative video camera, and IKEA was not just a creative idea (we'll return to this) – they were both radical breaks with how people understood a product, business and industry.

But how can you discover these opportunities for radical breaks? In this book we'll work with a five-stage model (see figure) that will detail how to take the steps that make this possible. Let us begin by going through the basics of this process – from imitating creativity to practicing dangerous thinking.

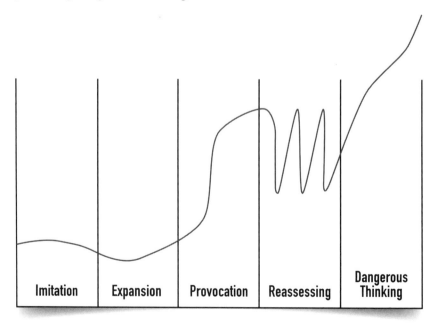

| Imitation | Expansion | Provocation | Reassessing | Dangerous Thinking |

Step 1: Imitation

The main problem with "creativity" is that human beings are innately good at *imitating*. In fact, we're so good at it that we barely notice when we're doing it. And things get real tricky when you start to realize that even the literature on creativity is mostly a question of imitating and copying other literature on creativity. It is in our nature to imitate: if we see a good idea our subconscious immediately sets out to replicate it. Even if it is an idea about creativity! In the video industry they had found a specific way to be creative, which hinged on adding more and more functions and design flourishes. There was a clear picture of what creativity was, and everyone tried to live up to this. Flip represented something that others in the business didn't even see as creativity, but something else, something threatening.

A great deal of creative work today, particularly in corporations (and books on creativity), is stuck in this phase. The problem is not that people aren't trying to be creative – because they are – but that without realizing it, people try to be creative *only in the way they know how*. Without really grasping it, they're often imitating earlier forms of creativity, as this is what they are led to believe they should be doing. Books on creativity tend to be about history and what worked earlier, and companies just sit there and listen. At the same time, the true innovators are already off, exploring strange, new trajectories.

Step 2: Expansion

Sometimes, we think that the way out of imitation is *expansion,* i.c., that we should increase our conceptual space. So we study other areas, collect more information, seek out more solutions. Many companies do this exceptionally well, and have gained a lot by doing so. But companies can also get stuck in this phase, without really understanding why they don't develop more than they do. Curiously enough, there are quite a few creativity pundits that myopically praise expansion. The problem here is that expansion, in itself, still takes place within our given framework – a little like improvising around a plan. Companies often like the comfort of this, as it is safe and well-known, and since it creates the feeling that the core is still intact and controllable.

We rarely reflect on the history of new business models, but these are often born out of something much more radical than just expansion. IKEA, the dominant giant of the global furniture industry, was one such radical break. When IKEA introduced the concept of cheap, DIY furniture, it did so in an industry that had expanded its horizons for a hundred years – new designers, new materials, new kinds of furniture. But no one had dared to think *dangerously* about the basic logic behind the product and the business idea itself. IKEA did so, and just like in the case of the Flip video camera, the reaction from the industry was one of shock and disbelief – even disgust. "Expanding the box" isn't nearly enough for seriously challenging the order of things, and we therefore need to look elsewhere for inspiration.

Step 3: Provocation

What Flip and IKEA did was that they didn't only look for creative solutions, i.e., imitate earlier ideas about creativity. Nor did they just expand upon old ideas. What they sought was something much more powerful, namely a radical *provocation* of existing thinking. Succinctly put, they did something that was seen as silly, threatening, dubious, unsuitable and impossible in a field. This is something quite different from just expanding horizons, and more closely resembles a reboot in thinking. Dangerous thinking starts with a provocative break – the moment when you introduce something that doesn't fit in to earlier frameworks and which therefore creates friction and discomfort. To make this step possible, we need to challenge the mechanisms that keep us in our comfort zone. To do this, we need to *challenge the "secret box"* (don't worry, we'll return to this) – this is the framework that keeps our thinking in check and under control. This isn't the same thing as "being creative", but a more radical confrontation with traditional modes of thought.

Step 4: Re-assessment

Once you've broken with your old frameworks, and thereby re-programmed your thinking, it becomes imperative that you *re-assess* much of the context within which you are used to working. We must start seeing creativity as something you work with continuously, rather than assuming that the break introduced in step #3 would be enough in itself. Dangerous thinking isn't a question of just getting a good idea, but of undertaking a continuous re-evaluation of the environment, a process of shifting perspectives. Organizations that want to become creative need to develop new ways of thinking. Creative thinking and creative leadership is not the same thing, but need to be combined to be effective.

Step 5: Dangerous thinking

Creativity should strive to become *dangerous thinking*. This is the level truly successful mavericks have achieved, and it is here we encounter the truly challenging, radical and revolutionary. This is creativity that doesn't fit neatly into PowerPoint presentations, creativity that shakes things up. As it is a little less easy to love, we often turn a blind eye to it. Still, this is the thing that sets apart the truly creative from the mediocrities. Flip was a form of dangerous thinking, and we'll discuss many other examples. To reach this level isn't easy, but the rewards can be great: dangerous thinking doesn't just generate ideas, it can change the world.

Working seriously with your creativity should mean breaking with the limitations inherent in steps #1 and #2. The transition can be tough, and re-assessing things can be a difficult process, but at the same time it is this very resistance that makes it all worthwhile. A process without resistance is a process without meaningful change.

The Four Parts of this Book

As may have become clear, this will be a book about how dangerous ideas are born, and how tough the process of thinking dangerously can be. Overall, the book follows the sequence described above, and progresses in steps from comfortable thinking to dangerous thinking. Every step is important, in its own way, but you should relate them to your own context.

Part 1: Comfortable Thinking and You

In the first part of the book we will look to how creativity has been turned into an uncreative, pale imitation of itself. It will show how our brain tricks us into thinking that we are creative when we really are not, and how many of the so-called "truths" peddled about creativity are nonsense. Our potential is greater than we're aware of, but also the risk of getting stuck in comfortable thinking is far greater than we tend to admit. So this is a call to action: we need to break with the comfortable! This part of the book corresponds with our first two steps, *imitation* and *expansion*.

Part 2: Provoking Thinking

Part two of the book is all about *provocation*. In order to change your thinking, breaking your brain's comfortable dependency on what it already knows, you need to subject it to provocation – creative shock therapy. "Exercises" in "creativity" aren't enough, far from it. To really get out of our comfort zone, we need to introduce some shocking notions. It ain't always nice, and sometimes it's downright unpleasant. But it is necessary if you want to push your thinking to the next level – the level of *dangerous thinking*.

Part 3: Reassessing the Context

In order to place our now more dangerous thinking in its right context, we need to look to how organizations can handle creativity. The usual fluff about how creative organizations are nice and lovely environments needs to be challenged, vigorously. Someone needs to dare to lead, to have the courage to take creativity that one step further. Real creativity needs to generate action, not just pretty ideas.

Part 4: Thinking Dangerously

At the end of the day, this book is about creativity as something that is dangerous. It is a celebration of ideas that do not fit in, that are seen as silly, laughable or dangerous, and that precisely because of this are exceptionally important. Not just good ideas, not just little things "outside the box". No, something much, much more.

Dangerous – as it represents a challenge

Thinking – as it questions our usual way of seeing things

Dangerous Thinking

PART 1

COMFORTABLE
THINKING AND YOU

"NOT ANOTHER BOOK ON CREATIVITY?!?"

It is the customary fate of new truths to begin as heresies and to end as superstitions.

—Thomas Huxley

Let's get the obvious facts out of the way, before we get down to the important stuff: creativity is important. We need it, desperately. It's the driving force in the contemporary corporation, a central part of the modern economy and critical for achieving individual excellence. Some even claim that it is necessary for humans to achieve balance and well-being. So of course it's important, and precisely because it is important this will be a book about how creativity can be developed, how companies can improve by working on their creative potential and how innovation actually happens.

But do we need yet another book about creativity? In my library I have hundreds of books on creativity, creative organizations, creative economies, innovation, business ideas and so on, *ad infinitum*. I have longwinded theoretical ones, short colourful ones, books that explain how creativity can make you rich, books on how creativity can save the world and books that mainly consist of pretty pictures. On my shelves I can find books on how creativity works in groups, on how to lead creative people, even books on how to raise a family with the help of creativity. Creative cooking, creative fitness, creative problem-solving, creative marketing – it's a never-ending list.

So what in the world could have prompted me to write one more book about creativity? There's a simple answer, but it's also a little tragic. Having read more than a hundred books on creativity and innovation, one thing became very, very clear to me: books on creativity are suffering from a serious lack of creativity. Succinctly put, they are far too similar, full of examples that are similar and over-used, and tend to reuse exercises in a way that might be funny if it was meant to be ironic. But it isn't. Books on creativity don't kid around, and take themselves so seriously that they at times become the very definition of uncreative. Book after book lines up the same examples, the same exercises, the same pompous statements. If there is one thing that the literature on creativity needs it's creativity, and plenty of it.

Just Say No!

As an example, take those goddamn nine dots…. I guess there must be one or two people who've never seen this (I think there are tribes in Borneo that haven't, and I envy them), but by now it must be a pretty small minority. In brief, the exercise starts when the author, in his most arrogant tone, presents a picture where nine points are arranged in a 3x3 matrix. The reader is then supposed to connect these by either four straight lines drawn without lifting the pen, or some variation on this sad theme (my favourite being the one where you insist you have do this with a single straight line, which you can do by cutting out the dots and arranging them in… a straight line). The exercise is trivial, overused, and not even particularly good for developing creative thinking. In itself it is completely uninteresting, but the frequency with which it is constantly reused is fascinating.

THIS SPACE IS FREE FROM TRIVIAL CREATIVITY EXERCISES
Figure 1.

If you look at what the books are really trying to say with this kind of exercise, it becomes obvious that they are put in to convince the reader that creativity is a kind of secret, a mystical form of knowledge that should be transferred from the more enlightened author to a slightly dim reader. There is in fact a very distinct sense of religious fervour in much of what is written on the subject, to the extent that it even scares me a little. Nor do I like the high-and-mighty attitude that colours much of the discourse: "Here's a riddle. Can you solve it? No? I thought so. Come here, my limited friend, and I'll show you just how silly you are…" (Later on I will do the exact same thing, but with the assumption that I'm no better, and maybe much worse.)

These exercises are a form of ego-boosting for the author, and not really ways to say anything interesting about creativity. And this becomes particularly clear when you notice that the same exercises are used in book after book after book! Just as I finished typing that sentence I hollered at my son, asking him to go to my bookshelves and get me three books with creativity in the title, just to test this out. Out of three randomly selected books, two featured the image with the nine dots.

The third, Mihaly Csikszentmihalyi's *Creativity*, did not – but it has neither pictures nor exercises. It does make up for this, however, by repeating several other things that are endlessly recycled in books of this type.

Write Your Own Creativity Book!

If it was only a single exercise that was repeated over and over again, one might excuse this. However, the fact is that most books on creativity look more-or-less alike, if with some modifications. In fact, you might even say they all just repeat a single model from 1926. This was the year when a gentleman by the name of Graham Wallas (1858-1932) created a basic model for the creative process, one with four simple steps:

- Preparation
- Incubation
- Illumination
- Verification

Since then, this model has been modified by hundreds of authors, through permutation after permutation after permutation. Some add a step or two, mainly by subdividing one of the above, and most give the steps new names. And yes, people might add a few things as to how preparation is supposed to be done, or talk about the importance of action in verification. They might even arrange the steps in a circle, so that verification is followed by a new round of preparation. Still, they keep to the script.

If they can do it, *so can you!* Just use the basic model above, give the steps funky new names, add a phase (whatever, it doesn't really matter), and put it in a nice, new colourful model. Why not in the shape of a shark? See, *you too can be a creativity thinker!* I mean, why not? A lot of people have already done it… Once you have your model set out, spice it up with a series of examples and exercises. If you can't think of new ones, just use the same ones you find in other books – everybody does it. Hey presto, you're finished! Now all you need to do is to compare your creation with a book you might already have on your bookshelf.

Did you find one? Let me guess: first the author spends a few pages arguing that creativity is really, really important. Then he or she runs through a series of chapters that outlines a series of things you need to do: you have to define the problem, preferably in several ways, and collect a mass of ideas and inputs while you're doing this. In other words, do what Wallas called preparation. Then you need to realize that creativity needs space, cannot be forced, and that naps are good. This is what Wallas called incubation. At some point, this will result in new ideas, even though the book will be quite vague about this bit. Wallas was refreshingly honest, and called this an "illumination", as he knew damn well that he really didn't understand it either. The ideas then need to be tested, evaluated, acted upon, that is, they need to be verified.

It's been the same pattern, over and over again, since 1926. A lot has happened since then, nations have risen and fallen, new industries have bloomed while others have gone bust, but the creativity books look a whole lot like they did way back when.

Creativity, Hallelujah...

It is thus a tragic but true fact that books about creativity are not particularly creative, and the reuse of exercises is only the most visible symptom of the greater problem. This, by the way, is an important part of how we've tamed and neutered creativity into something taken for granted, a series of anecdotes to tug at your heartstrings. Most, if not all, books on creativity spend a lot of time yammering on about how important the subject is, how creative companies are more successful than uncreative ones, and how much happier you could become if you'd just dedicate yourself to creativity. There is something fanatical in the way they nag at the reader about this, in how they *demand* that people have to accept creativity into their lives. Oh, and how they more or less implicitly state that those who aren't prepared to do so are failures and losers.

Here, the religious tone that is present in much of the creativity industry comes very much to the fore. You either get it, or you're a lost soul.

Organizations that haven't seen the light are wrongheaded, and should be either converted or humiliated. And you're not supposed to question creativity. Never, ever, ever are you encouraged to do so. The righteous missionaries of this particular cause really can't give an answer when you ask them if things couldn't work with a little less fervour and frenzy, but neither are they ready to accept any criticism or competing perspectives. For most people writing on the subject, creativity is just as holy as even Jesus, Buddha or Allah, so you can be critical about everything as long as you're not trying to be creative about creativity. It's an all-encompassing faith where creativity is the great unquestioned good.

The problem is that I can't really accept this. I am a born sceptic, and this also means that I take sceptical view of the notion of creativity. I don't accept the argument that creativity can solve all problems. I don't think that an organization with only creative people is a good idea, or even possible. Call me a cynic, but I'm not even convinced that creativity is always a good thing. On the contrary, I can easily think of many situations where creativity is a really bad idea. *But creativity has become a church,* and in it this kind of blasphemy is not accepted, so as one of the heretics of creativity I have found myself crankily standing on the sidelines of a field I really want to like and enjoy. But this is not only a bad thing, and as Art Kleiner argued in his book, *The Age of Heretics,* we need such thinking to develop what we have.

> A heretic is someone who sees a truth that contradicts the conventional wisdom of the institution — and remains loyal to both entities, to the institution and the new truth. Heretics are not apostates; they do not want to leave the "church". Instead, they want the church to change, to meet the truths that they have seen halfway.
>
> —Art Kleiner

Reclaiming Creativity

So, as a heretic, I love creativity. This might sound odd coming from someone who has just spent a few pages to harshly criticize it, but the fact is that I am enamored and fascinated by creative thinking, creative people and creative organizations. The problem, however, is that I refuse to accept simplified and reductionist descriptions of this strange, odd, messy, contradictory, mischievous and chaotic field. For me, this is something very different from the altogether proper, well-behaved and clean-cut thing that one is normally served in books on creativity. For real creativity isn't something neutered and servile. Instead it is unabashedly improper, frequently dangerous, and often more than a little uncomfortable. Many of the people trying to sell creativity (and we are talking about salesmen here), seem to see it as a kind of jazz – nice to listen to, often a little surprising but rarely shocking. Something like conceptual muzak, inoffensive and devoid of soul. I prefer to see it a little differently. To keep to my metaphor, I see real creativity as the kind of music adults get annoyed at kids for listening to – punk, death metal, gangsta rap. Different, radical and frequently offensive.

And so to this book. It is based on my work on creativity and innovation over the last decade, work conducted both in practical collaboration with corporations and organizations, as well as in the more conceptual sphere. Over the years, I've become increasingly dedicated to injecting a little creativity into the discussion on creativity and innovation, and to finding ways in which these concepts can regain a little of the unbridled energy that is supposed to define and infuse them. As I see the world, creativity is not made of just pretty things and nice sentiments. Instead it is something that can be dirty, mean and raw – *something that actually changes things.*

Creative Delinquent

So, creativity is an unkempt delinquent that picks his nose and puts his dirty shoes up on the table, not a well-mannered youth with bright eyes and a winning smile who retells popular anecdotes so that the audience will like him. As I see it, creative people have enemies, and this isn't only a good thing, it is how things are supposed to be. Why? Because if everyone likes what you say, you can be damn sure there's something wrong with the message – it doesn't question assumptions, it doesn't challenge anything. In a word, it is safe, and safe is the enemy of creativity.

This book will try to combat this, and introduce a strange new world of creativity. It will be a world where the repulsive, the filthy, the silly, the ugly and the childish are things we need more, not less, of. It will be a world where a book on creativity quite aggressively tries to be contrarian, even towards creativity. With this in mind, I really, really hope that not everyone will like what I write here. In fact, I would find it a failure on my part if no one gets mad, or upset, or both – at some of the things I write. So, I will really try to be a bit mean and disrespectful, uppity even. In all likelihood, I'll contradict myself more than once. And my fondest wish is that I manage to get at least one person nauseous in the course of this book.

Consequently, this will be a book about boundaries, about crossing over and exploring such, but also about how one can be tricked into believing one has crossed one. At first my plan was to write an ironic book about how to become a creativity guru, a manual for the person who wanted to fake creativity, but then I realized this would be far too cynical. So instead I decided to write on the real possibilities of critical thinking, about the strange things that happen when we really push thinking outside its comfort zone. So we will talk of things such as comfort, and feeling at ease, and being stimulated, and other horrible and mind-destroying things. But we will also talk about important things, such as how disgust, foolishness and imitation can break with the hidden limitations that make our thinking too comfortable for its own good.

This will be a book about boundaries, about crossing over and exploring such, but also about how one can be tricked into believing one has crossed one.

The point of this will not be to denounce creativity: quite the contrary. Instead, this is something we have to do in order to take creativity seriously, beyond the motivational poster and picture book fantasy. The thing is, I am in fact a true believer in creativity, and the possibilities inherent therein. I would love to see a world where creativity – the real, serious kind – had better opportunities to be heard, and where the joy of creating had better support and was more widely understood.

But at the same time I am a realist, and know that the road to such a world is much more difficult and winding than we'd like to think. If we want to make such a world possible, even in a local context such as within a company, we have to test a number of boundaries and cross these boundaries many times. To make these movements possible, I believe that it is of utmost importance to challenge our own thinking, to challenge what we believe creativity is and is not. We even need to challenge the necessity of crossing boundaries, so as not to make this an end in itself. This approach is inherent in dangerous thinking, and to properly understand it, we need to accept it as a double movement – one that both loves and challenges.

Uncomfortable Yet? Great!

We're all limited in our thinking, and all of us have limits to what we can think and imagine. To believe anything else is just naïve. Sure, we can challenge boundaries, but when people talk about breaking with frameworks and thinking outside the box, it is usually just empty talk. We need frameworks – a box – for thinking to be possible. Without our boxes, we're lost at sea, as all thought builds on frameworks, assumptions, accepted conventions and definitions.

The problem is not that we have boundaries in our thinking; the problem is that we are rarely aware of where the real ones are. And the only way to find these boundaries, to really come to grips with what they are, is to cross them. Sure, this is exactly what creativity gurus at every creativity workshop or trivial creativity exercise claims to achieve, but they tend to be wrong, dead wrong.

> Without our boxes, we're lost at sea, as all thought builds on frameworks, assumptions, accepted conventions and definitions.

Basic creativity exercises – the usual talk about creativity being important/fun/valuable/whatever – doesn't work, not really. This is because the brain (a wily creature we'll discuss at length) immediately sees them for what they are. Our brain is amazingly proficient in handling these kinds of threats and challenges, and to do so in a manner that ensures that the actual barriers for creative thinking aren't questioned or even approached. In the same way certain kinds of stimulus can trick the brain into thinking that it is making independent decisions – see, for example, *Yes! 50 Secrets from the Science of Persuasion*, by Goldstein, Martin & Cialdini – creativity exercises can trick us into thinking we've become more creative when the real outcome is our mind has merely been flattered.

To work seriously with creativity we need to employ something more powerful. We need to bring in the big guns. Creativity isn't supposed to be comfortable or pleasant, and sometimes it can be quite disturbing. If a creativity exercise makes you feel good, this isn't proof it is working: it just shows that your brain is releasing endorphins as a reward for not challenging it. Enjoying creativity is the same as turning it into a safe, comfortable thing, and your brain is complicit in this deception.

By contrast, real creativity is the name we give to a transformation of thinking, a real change in how you view the world, and as with all serious changes, the process is never painless. So to talk seriously about it we need to go beyond the feel-good exercises, the funny anecdotes, and the general heartwarming sense of comfort that surrounds the modern discourse on creativity. Instead, we need to venture into spaces where things are uncomfortable, even scary, and where our normal techniques of mental navigation no longer apply.

We need to venture into spaces where things are uncomfortable, even scary, and where our normal techniques of mental navigation no longer apply.

If we can do this, if we can leave behind our sense of comfort and the glossy picture book image of creativity, then we will find that we can accomplish amazing things. The road towards dangerous thinking won't be easy, for nothing worth doing is ever easy. I've already stated than an idea without enemies is probably not a very good idea, for the simple reason that any challenging idea will by its very nature have opposition. In the same way, the seriously creative has to be difficult, because it must challenge the popular and well-known, make us uncomfortable, shake us free from our beloved sense of comfort and content. *Difficult, unpopular and uncomfortable – THIS is a motto for creative thinking worth taking seriously!*

WHY CREATIVITY?

Creativity is a bloody nuisance and an evil curse that will see to it that you die from stress and alcohol abuse at a very early age, that you piss off all your friends, break appointments, show up late, and have this strange bohemian urge (you know that decadent laid back pimp-style way of life). The truly creative people I know all live lousy lives, never have time to see you, don't take care of themselves properly, have weird tastes in women and behave badly. They don't wash and they eat disgusting stuff, they are mentally unstable and are absolutely brilliant.

—Toke Nygaard, design maven

We might start by asking the question: do we need creativity at all? Such a question will, without any doubt, be seen as heretical, even dangerous, and I can imagine that quite a few of my colleagues in the field of creativity will find it highly offensive. More to the point, they'd probably get riled up enough to go into a heartfelt speech about how "creativity is necessary for everything and everyone", and it "being the only thing from which we can build anything of value", as well as "being a key part of the very thing that makes us human". And a lot of other things, preferably **In Bold Capital Letters.** The problem is that I can't really take them that seriously. It is strange that so few of them challenge these conventional notions of creativity – particularly as so many of them spend their days telling their audiences that everything should be challenged. Everything, that is, except our ideas of creativity.

If you think about it, this is really odd. No sane human being believes that a car salesman extolling the car he's trying to get you to buy is doing it for any other reason except to sell, just as we know that a person selling a house is prone to showing it in the best possible light. But when people who make a living by talking about creativity launch into their normal spiel, the one about how creativity is beneficial and nice and lovely, we tend to accept this without really challenging it. No one kicks the tires of a creativity consultant, but what do we expect them to say, really? Just like professors in entrepreneurship tend to agree that the thing they are studying is important and worthy of study – and I should know, I've been one – most people who talk about creativity say little more than creativity is exceptionally important. They are victims of a curse, the curse of having to love that which they are dependent on.

Similarly, you can see in the public discussions regarding creativity a lot of talk, but not a lot of debate. Every single voice, every single statement is one more addition to the tapestry of agreement, one in which we can all agree that creativity is important, needs to be supported, must be boosted, and so on. Sometimes this becomes comical, as when government bureaucrats proclaim that we need more creativity, whilst they busily rubber-stamp yet another pile of edicts and instructions. Or when you realize that there are government agencies for innovation, which sounds a lot like setting up improv-studios for bureaucracy. The word is used as a mantra or an invocation – people seem to think that just mentioning creativity often enough will make it appear out of thin air, like an angel or a demon. Mostly, however, this uncritical adulation just makes me tired. Like the liturgy of a church, it can be pretty and even give you a sense of contentment, but when it just becomes words and dogma and ritual, that's when we need something a little more… heretical.

The Soviet of Creativity

When I'm out lecturing, I often tell the story of an academic conference on creativity I once had the misfortune to attend. I start by telling a joke, asking whether people can define a creativity conference. When they can't, I do it for them: "It is what you get when you gather a hundred middle-aged, white men in a room and they all agree with each other that what they are doing is really important."

The conference in my story was exactly like this. Even more dreadful, one of the keynotes was given by a Very Important Creativity Person, who also agreed with everyone there, but just so much more so. He burst on the scene, fists pumping, asking us if we believed in creativity. In fact, he sounded like a preacher addressing his flock: "Do you beli-i-e-ve in creativity?!" And yes, the flock answered as only the true believer can, with perfect agreement. Yes, they believed. For me, the only thing I could think of as I sat there was that scene from the movie, *The Life of Brian.* If you've seen the movie, you know what I mean. Brian, the hapless hero who was born in Nazareth at the same time as Jesus, is, in a pivotal scene, mistaken as a potential messiah. In order to sort out this tricky situation he tries to talk sense to an adoring crowd, telling them that it is stupid to follow him, reminding them: "You're all individuals!"

And without missing a beat, the crowd intones: "We're all individuals…" All except for one crusty old man, who screams: "I'm not!"

The joke is, of course, that the only true individual in the group was the man saying he wasn't: and at that conference I understood him perfectly. If this was what being creative meant, I didn't want any part of it.

This might sound a little cynical. There is of course plenty to like in creativity, and I don't want to badmouth it, not really – and you, dear reader, will have to decide whether this means that I, too, am compromised by the field I am in. Creativity in itself, when you engage with its true nature (warts and all), is still interesting and worth taking seriously. If we look at it in practice, in both business and in other spheres, it still holds that creativity is one of the most important functions of progress we have, a necessary part of all living social systems – an omnipresent aspect of human thinking and being. Another way to say this is to state that creativity is always present, in any situation. One of the great hoaxes is the way in which some pundits in the field have – through implicit threats and by raising uncertainty and doubts – made it seem as if creativity could die. Fear not, this isn't possible, save by eradicating all of humanity.

Eastern Bloc Entrepreneurs

Together with my exceptionally creative colleague, Saara Taalas, I once wrote a provocative article that in all seriousness stated that the Soviet Union, this odd parenthesis in world history, was the most entrepreneurial society the world has ever seen. How could we make such a controversial claim? Obviously entrepreneurship in the more traditional sense was illegal – together with much else – but there was still an exceptionally active sense of individual opportunity-seeking present in this strange society. The reason for our claim was simple: since the planned economy of this gigantic country messed up so regularly, and since even the simplest of products might be impossible to get hold of through the official channels, every single Soviet citizen had to become a highly creative economic agent. You could say that they all had to become entrepreneurs of their own lives – everyday opportunity seekers.

For instance, a person working as a butcher had to utilize his or her privileged access to meat in a way that ensured that they could obtain other products, at least if one wanted to make ends meet. The pharmacist, the seamstress, the factory worker at a car manufacturing plant and the functionary at Aeroflot all had to do the same. Everyone hustled a little (or a lot) in order to get things to work and try to arrange some small extras. In the end, this secret, grey economy (not to be confused with the black market) became a support structure for the planned economy – helping the latter to survive years and decades of severe mismanagement.

Put differently, not even the massively repressive Soviet state managed to do away with the creative economy, and this is a key lesson to learn about creativity. Even though tales about creativity used for survival aren't quite as straightforward as those of entrepreneurial youths engaging in it for fun and profit, taking creativity seriously requires we open up to the fact that it can emerge in contexts that we are uncomfortable with.

In entrepreneurship research one differentiates between survival entrepreneurship and capitalizing on new opportunities in the marketplace. The latter type loves to promote entrepreneurship, for these involve stories that are fun and motivational, even comforting. Here we have people who think up challenging stuff, who push the envelope, and who get richly rewarded for doing so. By contrast, in survival entrepreneurship we have people who just work hard and start companies because they have to. More boring? Absolutely. Less hip? Definitively. Still, their example is more common, and much closer to the norm, regardless of whether they represent the story people want to hear.

The point I'm trying to make is that creativity is always there, always a part of our lives. It raises its head during times of war, when people need to find ways of surviving. It turns up in prisons and POW camps. It can be found among the junkies on the urban sidewalks just as often as in ad agencies with ironically retro names. And it is this unrelenting energy, this power that permeates all human activity, that interests and fascinates me – not the glossed over publicity shots.

A World of Possibilities

On its most fundamental level, creativity is not about creating value or doing things in novel ways. It's not even about knowledge and its use. Instead, creativity is about seeing potential in the world, about being open to possibilities. Now, some of these possibilities are less than nice, some are improper and not for public consumption, and some are definitively X-rated. Many of them are unsuitable as motivational tales published in glossy magazines, but they are still there. Creativity deals with all the different ways in which people can enact things (or, in some cases, choose not to), and this includes all the solutions that human nature can bring to life when constraints restrict our possibilities to act freely. On one level this means that we can state that creativity is not an issue of needing it or not, as it simply never is a question of choices. Creativity doesn't care about our wish for it or our need – it is just there, even if it is sometimes just a quiet presence in the background.

The continuous and necessary presence of creativity means that thinking about it is not merely an issue of studying what can be done and what can be created, but also a case of researching the impossible and the destructive. Joseph Schumpeter, the famed Austrian political economist, is today best known for his concept of creative destruction. With this he wanted to communicate that all action that creates also changes the world, and thus also destroys. Because of this, we cannot just look to what is new if we want to understand the dynamics of creativity in the world. Schumpeter's insight was to see how creativity is always connected to change, and that this process contained a complex interplay between creating and destroying; in such a situation the context and that which is being destroyed becomes important to consider. Somewhat more succinctly put, we cannot treat creativity as only something perennially pleasant and productive, nor expect that things will turn out fine as long as we're "working more with creativity". Creativity involves change and destruction, too.

Why Do We Need to Change Things?

This is why, when I work with corporations that want to change and become more innovative, I often start off by challenging prevailing assumptions but then turn the tables by demanding that the company argue for their desire to change. At one point, I worked with a small but successful management consultancy who wanted to run an away-day focusing on working in a more creative manner, all in order to change the organization into something more edgy and hip. We worked through a series of creativity techniques, went through the possibilities they saw and the ones they didn't, and brainstormed all over. Tons of ideas were generated, many of them exceptionally interesting. There was a lot of enthusiasm in that room, but at the same time there was a feeling of it all being a bit forced. So I sat down with key personnel and asked them why they wanted to change the organization. I remarked that a lot of what they wanted from the company was already there, present and ready to be used. Many of the ideas had to do with individual dreams, and was proof of the engagement people had.

Over all, it seemed that the strength of the company was their culture and the way they were keen to take things on. Simply put, people seemed to like working there, and in this day and age this is not something to sneeze at. So I asked: "Aren't things pretty good the way they are?" The surprise etched onto the faces looking at me told me all I needed to know. They had never even considered that their current way of working, their well-functioning culture and their enthusiasm was enough. I remarked that change, even though we've been more or less brainwashed to assume it as a necessary and positive thing, can have a remarkable number of negative consequences.

So sometimes *not changing* might be the only smart choice. Still somewhat dazed, the people in the organization agreed that this sounded like a good idea, and stated that they had just become so convinced that change and creative choices were necessary that the thought had simply never occurred to them.

Symbolic Creativity and Real Creativity

There are two things to note in this little tale. One is that the company, in its mad daze to just do *something,* had forgotten to think about the possibility that things were OK as they were, i.e., the thought of not changing had become a **creative impossibility.** We'll return to this concept, as it is central to understanding the difference between symbolic and real creativity. The second is that the company hadn't thought through all the things that creativity might bring into the equation, and instead taken "creativity" simply as a label for everything they thought might be progressive. Rather than taking creativity seriously, as a process that both creates and destroys, they had assumed that the pretty pictures in books on creativity was all there was to it.

So when I pose the question, "Why creativity, and what creativity?" this is not only an attempt to provoke, but a challenge to people to think about what they mean with the statement, "I want to become more creative." What do *you* expect to get out of this process? Probably something like "good ideas", or something similar. Still, if we're to take creativity seriously, we need to be attuned to the fact that friction, resistance and destruction are also part of the package. Every great idea bares the seeds of destruction, for this is what makes it powerful. We often ignore or shy away from these aspects of creativity, but this does not mean that they're not there. In fact, these aspects may be the very thing we should focus on.

Missed Opportunities

How can we be more creative in how we think about creativity?

Also, what type of creation are we talking about? It can't be just about the things we happen to view as good or desirable right now, not if we want to be objective and open about it. Most, maybe all, truly creative ideas have been viewed with suspicion and fear when they were first introduced, so why should things be different now? When the internet was first introduced, most people did not view it as a creative idea. They saw it as a waste of money, a silly toy, an obsession that was only for icky nerds, and so on. And the people who thought this weren't idiots, they were people like you and me, people who wanted to be creative, wanted to innovate. They just didn't see what they were looking for in the internet, for they were looking for something that would live up to their ideas of the great and the good, and all they saw was something silly and foreign to their sensibilities. What is the lesson in this? If we only aim for an image of creativity that pleases us, and think only of those things we desire and wish for right now, we are in fact ignoring the real potential of new ideas, and making ourselves less creative in the process!

In other words, and stated more directly, we need to rethink the very core of the creative endeavour. If you want to become more creative, you need to ask the much more fundamental question: *how can we be more creative in how we think about creativity?* And in order to do this, you may well have to give up quite a number of cherished notions about the creative process.

THE CREATIVITY HOAX

The most annoying thing with many discussions about creativity is that so much of the talk is like cotton candy. Fluffed up, airy, with a sweet (if slightly sickening) taste, and if you try to poke at it a little you'll soon find that there is very little of substance behind all the pretty pink stuff. It's hard to dislike cotton candy, though. Many of us buy it almost without thinking when we go to the fairground or theme park, as it is just one of those experiences you like to repeat. Cotton candy is a kind of comfort food, and so is creativity talk. However, I sometimes wonder if it's all just that: a fun experience, lacking any real depth. Discussions about creativity often feel like an idea inflated far beyond reason, with the helpful aid of a lot of hot air. The people talking enthusiastically about creativity are in all likelihood honest in their excitement, and truly believe in what they're saying. But at the same time it is a fact that much of the discussion is full of empty clichés, fluff, bullshit and something very close to pure humbug. If we want to learn something about real creativity, we need to look beyond the usual discussion.

As previously noted, your brain is one shiftless organ. It's exceptionally prone to uncritically accepting anything it recognizes from before, and it is very, very good at buying into the same hoax over and over again. It might be a question of being fed the same old stuff about creativity, or the same old stuff about strategy, but the brain is still quick to accommodate and buy it. This tendency is the foundation of quite a large part of the creativity industry, and provides work for a number of creativity coaches and the like. They know (unconsciously, or at least I hope so) that you are culturally programmed to react positively to certain statements about creativity, and they are prepared to feed these to you over and over again. This is why the same examples and the same cases are repeated so often, to sometimes nauseating effect. So they repeat (for the 14,329th time) that it is important that creativity is not just an issue to be talked about, but also acted upon.

And everyone nods in agreement.

They say that we must allow ourselves the joys of failing.

And everyone nods.

They point out that life at the office becomes much more fun if people get to be creative at work.

And everyone nods.

Then they ask whether people feel their company supports creativity, and everyone shakes their head. Coffee, and start over. Yes, it's another productive day in the world of creativity coaching.

Your Brain is Shiftless and Lazy

Now, one of the reasons this state of affairs can continue is because a specific aspect of your brain's laziness is its capacity to trick itself into thinking it is developing when it isn't. When it is subjected to unfamiliar stimuli, such as a new exercise or brain-teaser, the immediate reaction of the brain is not to respond creatively. Rather than trying to solve the problem in a new way, the brain's habitual reaction is to see how it can utilize its old bag of tricks. This often means that time spent trying to stimulate creativity with clever exercises mostly results in the brain *actively avoiding development,* i.e., surviving on the basis of what it already knows.

Over the years, we've been inundated with reports of just how brilliant and complex the human brain is, what a magical machine we all carry around. And there is a lot of truth in this, the brain is a wondrous construction. But this does not mean that it is always working for our benefit. In his book, *Kluge: The Haphazard Evolution of the Human*

Mind, Gary Marcus, who is a professor of psychology at New York University, has argued that much of our cognitive apparatus is in fact a rather clumsy construction, one where a number of mechanisms that might have had immediate use in pre-historic times can actually harm our thinking today. What he, together with a number of prominent psychologists has noted is a very simple but often forgotten fact – that the brain is a biological thing, and thus bound by biological/organic constraints. Sometimes, people say that the brain is a muscle, and this is very true. But just like a muscle, the brain is designed to conserve energy, and thus not exert itself more than is necessary. The first rule of any biological organism is to try to expend as little energy as possible.

So when the brain encounters something new, it will try to find the simplest solution, the easiest fix. Most creativity thinkers acknowledge this, and try to utilize exercises to jog the brain beyond this point. But they underestimate the capacity of the brain to adapt to circumstances.

Workout or Sunday Stroll?

Anyone who has become serious about physical exercise knows that the body can very easily become accustomed to a specific kind of effort, and that in order to develop one needs to find new ways in which to shock the body – if you just keep to the same fitness regimen year after year, you might as well stay on the sofa. The same goes for the brain, yet very few people are prepared to put the same kind of effort into developing their thinking as they do keeping their body fit. And just as we are all really good at fooling ourselves into believing that a short walk will allow us to eat that extra doughnut, we often fool ourselves into thinking that a few quick mental exercises and a little doodling in a notebook would be enough to keep our creative abilities fighting fit.

Sadly, this is a hoax, and a big one at that. You won't become more creative by exposing your brain to play and games, but by forcing your brain to do things that it feels are different, uncomfortable, and tough. Your brain develops when you subject it to serious resistance, in the same way as you build stamina by running long distances often, not by taking a Sunday stroll. Neurological research clearly shows that it is in situations that are unknown and complicated for the brain to manage that there is a chance for it to develop new ways of working. Even if it is possible for the adult brain to create new neural connections and activate dormant parts of itself, this will occur in situations where the brain is forced to manage uncomfortable resistance rather than in the easy environment of the creativity workshop. What today counts as "thinking outside the box" is normally a comforting activity for the brain, a stroll rather than a proper run. The brain, in order to protect itself from undue exertion, creates something we could call a "box within a box" – a technique which enables us to fool ourselves into believing that we're breaking with old frameworks in our thinking when we're really just faking it.

We could compare this with how the body during a run can create the sensation of "the wall". This is a feeling that one simply cannot run further, and can feel a little like dying. Yet, it is one that can be transcended by a runner, and when you push yourself through the pain barrier you can normally run far, far longer than you might have thought possible. It is a *kluge* (clever mechanisms) the body has developed to conserve its energy, but a surprisingly powerful one. And the brain has not one, but several, of these mechanism to protect itself.

Later on in the book we will look at ways to subject the brain to the kind of resistance that can force it to develop, and talk about why it is important to make creativity something you work continuously with – a creativity regimen. Right now, the important thing is to realize that creativity and its development represents a challenge, can be a really difficult thing to engage with, and demands that you work with it. Sadly, you need to leave the notion of a quick and easy solution behind you.

Differences Exist: Deal With It

Similarly, one of the great illusions is the notion that everyone can be creative. This might be true on one level, in that one can get most people to develop their thinking and their creative potential in some way. However, on another level, the notion that everyone can be creative is simply untrue. Creativity is a little like the art of running quickly, in that it exists as a relative competence. If we look at athletes who run in the Olympic Games, we're not that hung up on the fact that they are all quick: we focus on the fact that one of them is faster than the others, and give him or her a medal to signify this. That the person who came last in the second trial heat is also really fast is not that significant.

In the same way, we might state that in all likelihood each and every person living today is more creative than most people were during the Middle Ages, but this does not in itself mean that we are all creative now. We can't all be "creative" at the same time, as there will always be differences and iconoclasts and outliers, people whose thinking differs from that of the general populace. What this means is not that people shouldn't engage with creativity, but that the dream of a perfectly dispersed creativity is impossible to attain.

We can all take steps forward, but we need to keep in mind the distinction between general development and the necessary differences between individuals. You, the reader, can become more creative than you are, but that doesn't necessarily mean you'll become "creative", for if everyone around you develops as well, you won't have gained any real edge. This is "the Red Queen Effect" (of *Alice in Wonderland* fame), where "[i]t takes all the running you can do, to keep in the same place."

In the contemporary world, with the pressure to develop innovative thinking, just doing it in the prescribed manner will only keep you on the same curve as everyone else, and some people will, by necessity, fall behind. So to really set yourself apart, it is not enough to attend the requisite workshops and play around with whatever the coach decides is the exercise of the day. Instead, you need to dedicate yourself to really challenging the issue, finding ways to think differently – even if this means abandoning what is seen as conventionally creative. At the same time we shouldn't get too caught up in our striving for one kind of creativity, trying to mimic and copy one specific idea of what this means. A big part of the problem is that we attempt to set up a defined goal, something specific that we want to get people to achieve. For people who are working with creativity and promoting it, such fixed images are important, but this does not mean that it is relevant for you. It shouldn't be!

Creativity and Power

The creativity industry has a power dimension, and in part works by stating that there is a better mode of being that people should aspire to, highlighting certain types of people and implying that these represent a superior type of human (cf. Richard Florida's notion of a "creative class"). Consequently, lectures and workshops on creativity can turn into rather worrying spectacles, since they often patronize and insult the audience. A classic technique here, often used by speakers, is to start out by talking about the importance of questioning everything, challenging all assumptions, and then talking about something else for a while – all in order to be able to turn the tables on the audience by suddenly challenging the audience as to why no one is protesting and questioning what you're saying. The speaker then smiles as widely as he or she can (going for the full-blown, shit-eating grin) and throws out his or her hands in a mocking gesture, to the embarrassed giggles of the audience. Yet again you've managed to establish a power relation, a position of dominance over the ones who are "just not creative enough".

Another way to achieve the same goal is to talk about yourself a lot, how you have motivated or changed the thinking of so many people, how people everywhere are responding to your message. Anything to establish that there is an ideal state, and to imply that the audience is not really living up to this – but simultaneously dangling the possibility that they can change, if they are only open to the message…. Don't misunderstand the point here. I'm not trying to claim that people who talk of creativity are consciously trying to oppress people, but rather that power dimensions exist in the creativity industry. Even though the intentions behind it may be good, the discussion about creativity has a tendency – even a need – to create a sense of exclusivity aimed at those who don't quite get it, those who aren't quite "there" yet. And all such constructions imply that those on the outside, these Others, are not quite as good as we are, and in need of development, illumination, or salvation – all available from your friendly neighborhood creativity consultant.

The Art of Always Being Right

Another strange power technique employed by writers is the art of always being right. This fine art hinges of there being a couple of fairly simple rhetorical tricks through which almost anything can be turned into "creativity". Key to this is a kind of shameless reversal manoeuvre, where everything can be turned into a creativity statement simply by praising some aspect of it.

For example: let us pretend you are a consultant, with creativity as a speciality. You've been tasked with leading a brainstorming session where a company in the IT business is supposed to generate ideas for getting more clients. The problem, however, is that the group is less than enthusiastic. We could even say they're trying actively to work against you, but little do they know I've trained you for this eventuality…. At first, they simply dismiss the whole exercise, and argue that there's no benefit in attracting more clients when they can't even deal with the ones they already have. Great, time to return that first hardball. Just exclaim: "Fantastic! You took the problem and you redefined it! Very creative."

Somewhat taken aback, the group decides to brainstorm anyway, but tries to throw you off by not taking it seriously at all, and instead begins discussing helping not-for-profits and doing this for free. You continue: "Brilliant!! You're looking for new business models and proactively building the company brand! Very creative."

Truly shaken, the group decides that this was a dreadful idea, but so is the IT business, and maybe the company should get into the used-car business instead, or maybe start selling T-shirts with rude messages. Besides yourself, you continue: "Excellent!!! You're thinking outside the box and trying to extend your competencies!! Very creative!" Repeat, incessantly.

See, you too can become a creativity consultant! *Remember to keep on talking, keep on agreeing, and keep on calling everything creative.* Never let on that you're just faking it.

Obviously I'm not saying that all consulting on creativity is this simple or simplistic. Still, in the mainstream thinking and writing about creativity there is a tendency to always find something to be enthusiastic about, something to applaud. Things in this strange world are simply a little too affected by the rose-tinted glasses we normally don when talking about creativity. It's all a little too simple, a little too self-evident. And things get really strange when we look at the examples people tend to use. In the same way in which an exercise can be repeated in book after book after book, the same companies and the same anecdotes can be recycled a hundred times without anyone batting an eyelid (my personal favourite being the endless and quite bizarre tendency to remind people that some hapless record executive turned down the Beatles, an example I've read so many times I get nauseous when I see it rehashed).

Right now, two companies have become the template that one seemingly cannot repeat enough – I am, of course, talking of Apple and Google, the poster companies for the "how creativity can make you a billionaire"-set. Apple in particular has become such a golden oldie in all kinds of business writing that I've started to suspect that some form of sponsorship arrangement might be in place. Things become quite hilarious when you consider that the company, during the time it became the icon of the creativity crowd, has been run by a man who made intolerance a management philosophy – as detailed in the book, *Inside Steve's Brain,* by Leander Kahney. I must admit that I'm actually quite charmed by Steve Jobs, if only for the reason that he so elegantly disproves many of the pet theories from the field of innovation and creativity research. But enough about him. Succinctly put, it is not just a question of creativity literature repeating sweetly romantic tales where things are just nice and fine and lovely, they also tend to do so about the same old things, to the point of absurdity.

Innovation or Imitation

Sometimes when I'm out speaking about creativity, I tell a story about the most insane innovation project I've ever seen. A major European corporation had asked me to be a speaker at their annual top management conference, an event where they presented the final results from their very expensive innovation project. This project had been initiated in order to make the company more innovative and creative in their approach to business, and was the current CEO's pet project.

The CEO ran the presentation, and proudly showed off all the wonderful things they had done, but with special emphasis on their travels to "leading innovative companies" in order to learn "best practice". In fact, he said, they hadn't just visited Apple, they'd gone to Google *as well!* After this, it was my turn to step up to the dais. I did so and began by softly remarking that innovation really is a strange and many splendored thing. Sometimes it meant that one tried to do what others did not. Here, it seemed to mean that one tried to mimic the same companies everyone else was imitating.... I never did get invited back.

There are many illusions in this strange business of creativity, and many ways to fool oneself, even if one has the best of intentions. But why do things turn out like this?

THINKING DIFFERENTLY ABOUT THINKING DIFFERENTLY

In contemporary society, creativity is discussed so much and so often that we rarely bother to try to define the concept, as it seems so self-evident what it means – and if you do wonder, there are tons of people about who are prepared to incessantly talk about, and define it, for us. So on some level definitions might seem unnecessary. However, if one considers it a little more closely, one realizes that creativity is a very strange thing to try to define. There is something paradoxical and ephemeral about it, something that makes it incredibly difficult to pinpoint – even when we feel it's all quite natural and self-evident.

If we look at creativity in an analytical manner, we very quickly end up in logical contradictions. Let's start from one of the most typical ways of defining creativity. Here, creativity is defined as the mental process(es) through which new ideas are born, more specifically so that creativity represents a process which enacts change and breaks with earlier frameworks. Creativity thus deals with breaking with an existing state of affairs while simultaneously creating something new. Obviously there are other definitions, and variations on this theme, but a lot of people seem to agree with such a definition.

> Creativity is defined as the mental process(es) through which new ideas are born, more specifically so that creativity represents a process which enacts change and breaks with earlier frameworks.

But here be dragons. For if this is the case, shouldn't a similar principle apply to creativity itself? If creativity is all about breaking with how we see things and the frameworks though which we understand them, shouldn't it follow that the process of creativity is also about developing new understandings of creativity, radically different from all earlier ones? Maybe even the very antithesis of our existing ideas about creativity? Why should creativity be the only thing one can't think critically about?

This is an issue very few of those who talk about creativity enjoy addressing, since it takes us away from the self-evident discussions and exercises, and instead leads us into strange and uncomfortable waters. If one tries to be creative here, one needs to ditch much of the self-assured swagger of the creativity cheerleaders, and instead face a situation where one needs to be much more critical – and this is much, much harder than just repeating the old chestnut that one should be thinking differently. In such a scenario we have to re-examine our assumptions, and it becomes a lot more difficult to maintain the cheery confidence where creativity, of any sort, is always a good thing.

If we assume that creativity deals with trying to find new ways of perceiving that which already exists, then we must at least entertain the notion that creativity sometimes might be all about becoming less creative. Does this strike you as odd? Think about it: if everyone tries to be creative and think of new ideas, doesn't it follow logically that the most creative thing to do in such a context is to consciously try to be less creative and instead utilize old ideas? Or, if you prefer a sports metaphor, if everyone is running in one direction, the most creative thing is not necessarily trying to do the same but faster, but run in another direction instead. If nothing else, this can serve as an excellent exercise in creativity – and a much more challenging one than messing around with nine spots and a pencil. If we talk about thinking differently, and everyone tries to do this, the winner will be the one who doesn't. *Creativity – just say no!*

Doubt!

To add insult to this particular injury, it would seem that the most creative thing one can do is to doubt creativity. In an age when everyone sings creativity's praises, being consciously non-creative might even be a radical act! Or, as I wrote in another context (and what is more suitable here than blatantly copying oneself?):

"[The] seriously creative person isn't necessarily the one who has the most ideas, or the wildest ones. Nor is it necessarily the most novel or the most advanced solutions that define creativity. Instead, what is characteristic for the truly creative individual is the capacity of not allowing oneself to be caught up in a singular mindset, neither when dealing with the problem at hand, nor when it comes to what creativity is 'supposed to be about'. My favourite anecdote about all this comes from the Soviet Union. For a long time, NASA was thinking about how to create the perfect 'space pen', a ballpoint pen that could write in zero gravity. A lot of really smart people generated imaginative ideas, and millions of dollars were put into its development. When they finally created a pen that worked in space, NASA thought it a good idea to share this, and let the Soviet space program utilize this 'superior innovation'. Proud smiles turned into puzzled expressions when the Soviets simply said that they'd run into the same problem, and immediately switched to using pencils.* Simple, functional, old, tried and tested. This, to me, is a much more creative approach than the research and development that NASA engaged in, because one *dared to ignore creativity!* This is also a case of thinking outside the box, as creativity in this context has *become* the box."

I hear you asking: how can anyone claim that creativity is the box? I mean, it's all about thinking out of the box, right? Yes, it should be, but it only works when we're sure about what the box is. Today, everyone promotes creativity, and it is difficult to find even a single individual that dares talk against it. I have in my own work dedicated a significant number of hours to going through corporate reports and whitepapers, all in the vain hunt for a single corporation who isn't stating that creativity and innovation are among the core values and critical elements of their over-all strategy. I've failed in this, but during my search I've managed to bag a much rarer beast. In fact, I have achieved something very few social scientists ever do – I've gotten the elusive result of 100 per cent.

---

* It is not entirely clear whether this story is factually true or not. In fact, pencils would probably be a tricky proposition in space. Shavings and broken tips would in all likelihood be problematic in a weightless environment, and might even constitute a safety issue (you don't want delicate instruments messed up with pencil shavings, particularly not in space). The truth is in all likelihood more complex than the story makes it out to be, but as an anecdote the tale of the space pen is fantastic.

It is an old truism in research that you can never get a result where the outcome is 100 per cent. This is because there is always some little snag, some variable. One hundred per cent should be an impossibility, as there simple never exists such sureness and certainty in the world; except when it comes to creativity (and innovation, its somewhat older brother). For if you ask about creativity and innovation, the fact is that every corporation and every CEO claims this is critically important, and one has to dig much, much deeper down into the organization to find someone to grumpily disagree and state that it's all mumbo-jumbo. Maybe. If you're lucky.

I can almost hear the creativity consultants protesting. Sure, they say, everyone's *talking* about it, but are they really doing it? Are they actively engaged in developing it? This is, of course, something one can argue about for quite some time, but such questions don't really address the issue at hand. We still live in a time where everyone professes a faith in creativity. We are living in a time when it is exceptionally difficult to find people who have the courage to criticize this viewpoint, who dare to question the way in which this idea has become seen as self-evident and universally accepted. And even if it might be true that not all those who promote creativity act accordingly, this doesn't alter the fact that there is an ideology of creativity, a dogma that holds creativity and innovation as pure and good and true, for ever and ever. Amen.

Beautiful and Beloved By All

Actually, things are even worse than I portrayed them to be. Were it just a question of corporations talking up creativity one might accept it as yet another management fad, but the sad fact is that the issue has become politicized to the core. Today, it is not only CEO's and consultants who hail creativity; it can just as well be a bureaucrat or a prime minister who's kneeling at this particular altar. If we look globally we can find that the Communist Party of China, drawing their inspiration from Mao, have stated that creativity is a natural part in the development of communism, and even a central part of the revolutionary ideal. Looking elsewhere, we can find that Valdimir Putin, not often mention as part of the vanguard of innovation, has declared that creativity will drive the new Russia – and if an old officer of the KGB says it, you'd better listen.

I've long looked for someone who I could trust to be a stable presence in the world, someone I know wouldn't go for creativity and innovation – if only to be sure that there is someone out there who could be counted upon to be complete conservative in matters of creativity. I thought I had found such a person, but once again I've been disappointed. The person I had tagged as this bedrock of conservatism was a gentleman by the name of Joseph Ratzinger. He seemed perfect, for not only was he German and working in the Catholic Church, he'd been the boss of *Congregatio pro Doctrina Fidei* – an organization better known under its former name, the Holy Inquisition. All this felt like a pretty good guarantee that this would not be a person looking for innovation, and when he became pope, and took the papal name Benedictus XVI, I assumed that he would be my bedrock of conservatism, a stable presence in a changing world. I was disappointed, sorely disappointed! Today, even the Vatican (!) has innovation programs, and has even introduced new compensation schemes for employees. So not even the Holy See is wholly free from the euphoria surrounding creativity; and then, truly, the last bastion has fallen.

While I was writing this, one more example popped up on my radar, an example that for me confirmed that the mania for creativity has truly become global and universal. Since I'm a firm believer in collecting influences from all over, I have a virtual subscription to news from North Korea, a place beyond the surreal, and in addition left in something of a time warp. So judge my surprise when in my newsfeed I find the following, frankly hilarious, piece of news: "Kim Jong Il, the leader of the Democratic People's Republic of Korea (DPRK), has urged industrial plants to introduce new technologies to increase output. [...] He also called on the workers to fully employ 'mental power' and 'collectivism' to increase output." I have to confess to laughing until I cried. Yes, even in the most closed dictatorship in the world, a country so closed, most of the populace know nothing of modern world history, according to official propaganda the omniscient Kim Jong Il is touring businesses with a message of creativity ("mental power") being the one true way.

A Swift Kick in the Ass

It is examples such as these that have made me convinced that we need new ways of approaching creativity, as the old ways have become feeble and weak through everyone repeating them like so much homework and dogma. It is examples like these that have made me convinced that the most important thing now is to *start thinking differently about thinking differently.* Partly, this is a question of the things I've already discussed, of not falling into the trap of developing the exact same kind of creative thinking everyone else does, and instead look towards alternative, less obvious paths. But it is also a question of developing our thinking by looking at the constraints in our thinking, those that we're normally blind to and which are therefore not taken into consideration when we try to develop the creative process. Since creativity has turned into something posh, something nice and sweet and socially upstanding, we've become much worse than we think at engaging with the less elegant parts of our thinking. Fearing that we might seem improper if we access the troublemaking parts of our brain, we're hindering creativity and limiting its development.

> Start thinking differently about thinking differently.

So rather than ask yet more questions about how we can extend our thinking, we should focus on the question: "What is it that we cannot think?" What things lurk there, beyond what we currently allow ourselves to see, in the areas beyond our existing framework and comfort zones? This is something quite different from talking about some damn box, or extending your box, or jumping in-and-out and back-and-forth from your box, or whatever silliness we can get up to with boxes. This is because all metaphors that describe the boundaries of our thinking start from the wrong premise. The right approach looks at the boundaries we currently do not know, the ones we're not aware of, the ones that aren't affected by trivial creativity exercises.

The usual approaches fail because they start from very traditional ways of seeing the potential of human thought: this method is hindered by implicitly accepting social and cultural limitations and going down the same paths of development already established. Consequently, thinking differently isn't necessarily a question of working with the thoughts and the ideas we already have, but instead exploring the thoughts we have difficulty formulating, the improper and less than elegant ones, the ones that don't even seem to fit the situation and discussion at hand.

Thinking differently isn't necessarily a question of working with the thoughts and the ideas we already have, but instead exploring the thoughts we have difficulty formulating, the improper and less than elegant ones, the ones that don't even seem to fit the situation and discussion at hand.

Research in the areas of neurology, psychology and socio-psychology have generated tons of interesting results, but for our purposes, two findings from these fields are particularly important.

1. As human beings we are exceptionally prone to overestimating our capacity for taking in new ideas and new information, and in parallel underestimate our propensity to structure these under the categories our mind is already equipped with.
2. The human brain is fundamentally lazy, and even though it has a fantastic potential for development, it will only engage if pushed. If left to its own devices, the brain will always go for the easier way, the comfortable solution, the well-known path – psychologists call this *cognitive fluency*, and understanding this impulse is critical for realizing how difficult it is to develop real creativity.

To develop a more creative way of thinking is thus not just about actualizing a latent talent, but is in fact more about fighting deeply rooted tendencies in our thinking, even going against our very neurological make-up. This makes hard work, as does managing to avoid the many, many ways in which our brain can trick us. Let's look at some of these.

YOU ARE A GOLDFISH

Real knowledge is to know the extent of one's ignorance.

—Confucius

I think that goldfish are happy, in their own little way. They don't have much in the way of memory, and no great expectations in life. Nor do they question things to any greater degree, and tend to accept things exactly as they are. We all know someone who is pretty much like that, people who just seem to coast through life without reflecting or worrying all that much. And at times we all have thought about how this must be a nice way to live. But we're different, or at least want to claim we are. No one wants to say that they live their life free of thought and reflection. No one wants to own up to being like a goldfish.

At the same time you – yeah, you, holding this book – are much more similar to a goldfish than you think. I'm not claiming you're unintelligent (all my readers are very intelligent people, and good-looking to boot), or that every time you turn around in your bowl, I mean apartment, you've forgotten everything and now see the world anew. Not at all. But despite all the ways in which you are smarter, more talented, more competent and more intelligent than a goldfish, there is something that makes you similar to one. Not just you and the goldfish, mind you, but all of us. When it comes to this one thing, I'm a lot like a goldfish too. For just like goldfish, none of us can really objectively perceive our own life-worlds.

A goldfish lives its entire life in water, and there is not a single moment when it isn't totally immersed in the experience of being in water. Still, if we were to ask a goldfish to explain what water is (and we assumed that it had a language and could communicate) it wouldn't be able to. For the goldfish, water is everything, the beginning and the end. If you take that away, not only does the world it knows disappear, life itself ends. There is nothing else for the goldfish. Water? For a fish this is something so all-encompassing and omnipresent that you can't even fathom it being a thing, since it is everything. But this doesn't just apply to fishes. In our own different ways, we all live inside a version of the goldfish's water, accepting things that are so self-evident that we simply cannot imagine them to be any other way.

By the way, is democracy a good thing? It might seem a bizarre question, both because the way it was framed (or abruptly broke a frame) and because it seems weird in itself. Of course democracy is good. Come on, what else is there? Dictatorships? Fascism? Yes, democracy is a good thing, but at the same time it is one of those things that are so obvious to us that we cannot really see them any longer. For example: we find it really difficult to understand how the people of Zimbabwe can tolerate a despot like Robert Mugabe, and we struggle to comprehend how totalitarian states can be established. Sure, we can toy with variations on democracy, such as demanding a civics test before you can vote, or changing the age limits for voting, or radically changing the way in which one votes, but the notion of giving up democracy seems so strange and alien that we cannot even fully formulate it. Democracy and the market economy and salaried employment and mobile phones and a thousand other things are so obvious to us, so ingrained in our lives, that questioning them seems not only odd, it seems meaningless. Why in the world would one question the point of mobile phones?

Our Secret Box

What we're witnessing here is the exceptionally important difference between *conceptual expansion* and *norm(ality) breaking.* To understand the difference, it is helpful to consider a few things about the human brain. Your mind, like any mind, has several types of barriers and limitations. Some of these are quite flexible and easy to shift, while others are much more fixed. With regards to the former, the brain is in fact full of them, and each time you see something new or experience a new way of doing things some of these limits are stretched – your conceptual space expands. This space could be described as the domain of your everyday thinking, and the expansion of this is a natural and pleasant process.

To see how this works, consider my relationship with ketchup. For a long time I assumed that ketchup was a condiment that is always and by necessity red. However, due to a little impromptu shopping in a speciality store, I came across both a yellow and a purple ketchup (the former a banana variety, the latter a product for kids), and suddenly my concept of "ketchup" was expanded. Before I ran into a purple version I never thought of considering colourized condiments, but now I can quite effortlessly think about green or blue or pink ketchup. But does this really mean that I've become more creative? Sure, I can consider new colour possibilities in the world, and this probably has some impact as to how I think about potential colours for soft drinks or book design or pharmaceuticals.

Granted, these are all good things. But how important is this kind of conceptual expansion? The fact is, it might be much less important than we tend to assume, even if this realization might upset us. Even though it is important to expand your conceptual space, there is the risk that we start to assume this kind of development as fundamental, when in fact it is quite superficial. Expansion is a slow process of learning more about that which you find natural and are prone to think of, and thus only a gradual development along a preconceived path. A more fundamental creativity lurks behind other barriers.

Boxes within Boxes

We might explain this by turning back to the old metaphor of the box, but taking this much further. We could then explain it by saying that your thinking is not merely an issue of one box, but of two, one nested within the other. Normally, you're only aware of the inner box, the one that can be "broken" by challenging it, while the other one remains closely guarded by your subconscious. Your awareness of the inner one explains why it is so simple to manipulate its boundaries, and why you are able to "think outside the box". It is the borders of this box you're normally playing with, and the expansion of this sphere makes it possible for you to think of blue ketchup or devising a fun new ad campaign. Any expansion of this box will create a sensation of having done something new and creative, and this is also the reason why most people who work on ideation projects focus on this lesser box. But this is not the core issue, nor the real problem. The key problem and central issue should be the deeper limitation, the one you're not aware that you have. We might call this *the problem of the secret box.*

This box (and please, do get your mind out of the gutter...) plays an exceptionally important part in developing our creative potential, particularly if we want to do this on a more fundamental level. This "box" – the concept is a clumsy one, I know – is our version of the goldfish's water, a further boundary beyond what we normally perceive as our limitations. While expanding our conceptual limits is a nice activity to engage in, one that we can do through play and games, shifting our more fundamental norms in thinking is much harder and less comfortable. This is also what links the two boxes, and why creativity exercises might, paradoxically, make you less creative. The fact is that the extension of the borders of the inner box, the work of conceptual expansion, might be a way for the secret box to *protect itself.*

Rather than struggling with questioning the secret box, the brain will engage wholeheartedly (mixed metaphor very much intended) in all kinds of pretend-creative exercises and games. By doing this, the brain can trick you into believing that it has done something productive, and generate endless amounts of mood-enhancing notions and feel-good ideas. All the while the secret box remains unchanged, unchallenged, and very, very safe. In much the same way as we might pick a diet soda at a fast-food restaurant, and thus feel that we're being at least a little healthy, the brain loves taking on simple creativity exercises to feel better about itself. As this involves no real sacrifice, and because it serves as a welcome distraction from engaging with a real change in thinking, the fast-food of creativity coaching will always be in demand, even if the superficial work of conceptual expansion has a rather limited effect.

Of Drugs and Octopuses

Can a goldfish extend its conceptual sphere? Probably not. But an octopus can! Interestingly enough, research into octopuses shows that they are more than capable of finding new ways to get to food they desire, or playing with a new toy, or finding novel ways to escape from an enclosure. They can, without overextending themselves, make a review of their possibilities, analyze their surroundings, and utilize this input to do new things, things they've neither done before nor been taught. In this way they are creative, in a limited sense. More power to them.

Just like octopuses, we humans also need to do this, to extend our conceptual borders, so that we don't get stuck in a rigid and limited view of the world. By extending our conceptual frameworks we can also generate new ideas, new business possibilities, develop better products and services, and so on. All of this, of course, is good and progressive. Still, it is not all there is, and particularly this is not all that creativity is. Being content with this is, in a manner of speaking, to show the ambition of a mollusc.

As previously stated, the brain is lazy, and defined by the fact that it, too, wants to conserve its energy. Provocative and challenging thinking is hard work, and the brain isn't necessarily keen on such wanton expenditures of energy. So it has its own little ways of keeping us in check, particularly one amazing trick that we've already touched upon, but which is simply too good not to pay a little more attention to. One of the most amazing drugs in the world is an all-natural product, and one that the body can generate on demand. It is called dopamine, and we're all junkies. And the brain knows this.

Don't Be Fooled

Now, the brain is very good at rewarding us when we are well-behaved. As long as we feed the brain with things that it can easily fit into its frameworks, as long as we do not tax it with things that are too complicated to accommodate, it will reward us with shots of dopamine. This causes a charming reaction in us. We *feel* like we're really getting things done, we feel smart, and just generally good all over. As it feels good, and as we like feeling clever, we start associating these little highs with "creativity". Simple creativity exercises are very good at this, at triggering these feel-good sensations, at keeping the dopamine flowing. It's a love-in. There is one problem, though. It might feel like creativity, but it is really not. Sometimes it is the opposite of creativity.

The thing is, the brain rewards us most when we stick to the rules, when we aren't challenging it to break with its basic assumptions. When we find ourselves dealing with truly provocative notions, the brain isn't as pleased as when we play nice. In fact, it starts to react quite negatively. No more dopamine for you! The pleasant drugs are cut off, and stress hormones come into play. The brain wants you to know that it's not happy, and if it feels bad, you should too. Real creativity can, in this manner, feel almost physically repulsive! Yes, the feel-good, cotton-candy creativity feels better, but the joy is an artificial one. Wily thing, the brain.

Another take on this same phenomenon is the afore-mentioned *cognitive fluency*. It might not be a surprise to know we prefer to think about things that are easy to process rather than those that are difficult to handle, but we often underestimate just how powerful this tendency is. Cognitive fluency affects a whole plethora of things in our thinking, including judgment, the way we choose between alternatives and creativity. When it comes to making judgments, studies have suggested that we tend to buy stocks and shares with easy-to-pronounce and easy-to-remember names, and that we find statements that are easy to process more convincing than those that take longer to get our heads around. Cognitive fluency works as an adaptive shortcut, an instinctive affinity for the familiar. In early human development, this made a lot of sense, as was pointed out by the psychologist Robert Zajonc: "If it is familiar, it hasn't eaten you yet."

Cognitive fluency means that when the brain has got used to something, it also becomes attracted to it. Familiar messages are easy to process, so the brain starts developing a preference for them. Things written or told in an easy-to-understand manner are not only picked up more readily by the brain, they are seen as more meaningful. Anything that will fit existing cognitive patterns will be given special treatment, which will affect judgment and decision-making in dozens of different ways. The effect on creativity should be obvious. It might seem counter-intuitive that a solution that we on some level recognize would, by the brain, be seen as more creative than a completely foreign one; but this is what cognitive fluency indicates. The brain has a bias for simplicity, and we're along for the ride.

Jazz Men

For some additional input into this, we can examine the study on creativity and brain functions that was conducted at Johns Hopkins University by Professor Charles Limb and his group. Using clinical trials, the purpose was to understand what happened inside the brain when a group of seasoned jazz musicians were asked to improvise on a theme, i.e., to think in new ways about a melody. You might assume that this feat, playing improvised jazz, would require increased activity in some part of the brain. As the study dealt with highly trained professionals, with thousands upon thousands of hours invested in their art, you would think that they could access their brains in a way that would make some creativity-lobe light up like the proverbial Christmas tree.

However, the evidence pointed in the opposite direction. Rather than increasing brain activity, the masters could shut down a part of their mind and fight back when the brain was trying to rein them in. More to the point, the study showed that when the musicians started improvising, they showed a marked decrease in activity in a part of the brain called the dorsolateral prefrontal cortex. This is the part of the brain that deals with organization and self-control, and *being able to quiet it seems to have a connection with the capacity to create.* In the fight between creativity and the brain, the jazz musicians had learned a trick of their own, one which enabled them to fight back.

Obvious?

One of the strangest thinkers of all time, both in general and within the sphere of economic thought, has to be the French surrealist, librarian, philosopher and unrepentant dirty old man Georges Bataille (1897-1962). Among his many, many writings we can find one called *The Accursed Share,* a very odd book that manages the considerable feat of thinking differently about economics. Here, Bataille shows how the usual way in which we understand economics – as the sphere of parsimonious and effective action – is in fact only a small part of the totality. The sphere of saving and optimizing is in his description *the limited economy,* and this only exists to enable the operation of *the general economy.*

This latter sphere is all about expenditure and waste, and Bataille remarks that if you analyze economics systematically, you will realize that the point of most economic activity is on a more general level, making our preferred forms of waste – war, spectacular celebrations, large government programs – possible. This waste is not negative in itself, as society needs a goal and something to strive for. If we all just tried to save as much as possible no development would ever occur, so one must realize that general expenditure is in fact the very engine of economic development. Without people who are prepared to expend resources and take the risk that all will be wasted (we often call them entrepreneurs), the economy would come to a standstill.

If we allow ourselves to draw comparisons, we can state that conceptual expansion, for all that it does and enables, fulfills an important function, but is still a limited rather than general form of creativity! The general form of creativity is not one of merry expansion, but one of breaking with what we see as normal, natural, suitable. It will always be a matter of norm(ality) breaking, of crushing the barriers in our thinking that guide what we tend to see as indisputably true or otherwise pointless to discuss since *that's… just… how… things… are…*

What the term "secret box" – which is the one that needs to be subjected to norm(ality) breaking – describes is the zone of your thinking within which your brain can still feel comfortable and complacent. This is the zone that remains unchallenged as long as you haven't broken with any central norm, the part of your brain that remains unchanged as long as you don't question what you think is natural and normal. Looking to the experts in this matter, we can refer to professor Claes Gustafsson, who in his book, *The Production of Seriousness,* has called this limit the "wall of the self-evident". In order to challenge this barrier one has to consciously dare to explore the ways in which thinking becomes uncomfortable – like the goldfishes, we need to critically examine the water around us.

The brain is an amazing organ, in many ways. One of its most amazing features is the way it can always convince itself that things are normal and just as they're supposed to be. Corrupt CEO's convince themselves that everyone else is doing the same thing, people who dedicate their lives to *Star Trek* become convinced that in a perfect world everyone agrees that James Tiberius Kirk is the pinnacle of human evolution, and the truly scary thing about the people who've been convicted of crimes against humanity is their insistence that anyone in their situation would have done the same thing. We are all world champions in the fine art of fooling ourselves, in making everything we do and think seem perfectly natural and sensible. This is important in order to build a stable identity, but at the same time highly limiting to creativity as it blinds us to what lies beyond. Real creativity exists in this new sphere, beyond the notion that what we think is good is in fact good, that what we think is natural is in fact natural, that what we think is normal is in fact normal. We're all brilliant in seeing our limited view as natural and

True, real, serious creativity is out there, and it lives on the other side of the wall of the self-evident.

self-evident. But we're wrong. True, real, serious creativity is out there, and it lives on the other side of the wall of the self-evident.

To get there, it is not enough to expand upon that which you already know, or to try to extend into spheres one can easily perceive. To break with the limitations of the secret box, you have to face your own deep-rooted limitations, and in a conscious manner explore the things one thinks are uncomfortable or unpleasant to think about. Since the secret box is defined by that which we are comfortable with, all forms of norm(ality) breaking have to deal with our natural desire to stay within our comfort zone. When you break with this you are confronting your own limitations, the guiding principles that normally dominate your thinking. Uncomfortable? Definitively, but also incredibly useful and empowering.

Lounging in Lagos

At times I get asked one very specific question, namely: "If you could go anywhere in the world to see the forefront of creativity, the future of the economy, where would you go?" Most people seem to expect one of the usual suspects, an answer like, "Shanghai" or "Seoul" or "San Diego". I've always answered "Lagos, Nigeria". This is for many reasons. For one reason or another, Africa almost never gets mentioned when creative economies are discussed. As a continent with more than 50 countries, a billion inhabitants and more than a thousand languages, Africa represents both an enormous problem and a fantastic possibility that we still know so very little about. It is a continent that at times seems to be locked into a perennial crisis, but which at the same time holds such enormous potential.

And Lagos perfectly encapsulates the whole continent. An unplanned metropolis with 8 million officially counted inhabitants (and an unknown mass of unofficial ones), with the fastest population growth on Earth – which the hyper-creative architect Rem Koolhaas has called the future of the city. A city where the almost complete lack of town planning has created such orderly and predictable traffic jams that these have become impromptu but highly functional marketplaces. A city where one of the biggest businesses is email scamming, but which despite this has managed to develop a booming movie industry, even when most movies are produced in a week with a budget of $20,000 US and are sold as DVDs at local markets for two dollars each. A city where creativity is not something you plan, but something that makes it possible to survive. The city is bizarre, chaotic, impossible – and thus of the greatest importance for the person interested in the truly creative.

Lagos represents a magnificent problem, something too complex to grasp but too large to ignore, something that should collapse under its own weight but which stubbornly just keeps growing. A strange place, with strange logics. A place that definitively isn't always nice and happy, but often scary and dangerous. Here we see creativity on the rough side of the tracks, a kick in the ass of comfortable thinking, a challenge big enough for a heretic. Strange, unconventional, impossible Lagos might not be the nicest place on Earth, but it might just show you the true face of creativity, working and living outside of the comfort zone.

So when, in the coming chapters, we engage with norm(ality) breaking, we will do it Lagos-style. We won't do it in an ordered, planned way, but by escaping comfort zones and attacking some of the norms that we naturally but unconsciously tend to guard fiercely. We'll move beyond cognitive fluency, and towards spaces that, just like Lagos, may seem threatening, provocative and uncomfortable.

The four areas of normalized thinking we'll start with are *the pleasant, the tasteful, the suitable* and *the serious.* And we'll demolish them all. Each and every one of these norms represents a barrier in your thinking, and demolishing them will open up vistas for your creativity you may never have been aware of. Each norm you break represents something much more profound than playing at being creative through little games. Each broken norm will force you to confront your own version of the goldfish's water; for you *can* become something more than a goldfish, if you want to. It won't always be easy, but it can be done.

PART II

PROVOKING
THINKING

IT DOESN'T HAVE TO BE NICE

> Like the fella says, in Italy for 30 years under the Borgias they had warfare, terror, murder and bloodshed, but they produced Michelangelo, Leonardo da Vinci and the Renaissance. In Switzerland they had brotherly love — they had 500 years of democracy and peace, and what did that produce? The cuckoo clock.
>
> —Harry Lime in the movie, *The Third Man*

In his bestselling book, *The 4-Hour Workweek,* Tim Ferriss recounts how he, as a rank amateur, still managed to win the Chinese Kickboxing (Sanshou) national championships. He entered on a dare, and had only four weeks to prepare. He could have practiced as much as he wanted, and tried to find some clever punch or kick that set him apart. Instead, he engaged in a bit of dangerous thinking. Realizing that he'd probably lose every single match if he tried to fight in the conventional way, he went and studied the rules. Here, he discovered two things. Firstly, the weigh-in for the event was the day before the matches started. Secondly, if a fighter fell out of the ring three times in a match, this counted as a technical knockout. So, what did Tim Ferriss do? Using dehydration techniques, he dropped a lot of weight just before the weigh-in, only to hyper-hydrate the weight back in time for the fights. This gave him a definite edge in sheer mass, and also made it possible for him to utilize a very novel technique. He fought in the style of a sumo wrestler in a kickboxing tournament, and proceeded to just shove his opponents out of the ring until he won on TKO (total knock-out). Despite highly annoyed – we might even say disgusted – referees, he won the championship using a single technique, the bully shove. Unsportsman-like? Yes, I think you could argue it was. Effective? Hell yes. Creative? Very, very much so. For creativity doesn't have to be nice to be effective.

As previously stated, creativity has become one of the business world's security blankets, a sweet old teddy-bear that everybody likes. No one has ever been fired for suggesting "creativity" as the theme for the corporation's yearly conference, and we all know that saying something about the need for more innovation in the company is a sure way to get people nodding and agreeing with you. A lot of people think that this is a very good thing indeed. Unfortunately, it is nothing of the sort. Instead, it's a dreadful thing, one of the worst things that can happen to the development of creativity. Making it something so controlled, so polished and housebroken is a surefire way of neutering it and taking away most of the things that makes it an engine of meaningful change. Creativity today has become a kind of elevator muzak, a bland replica that doesn't offend or challenge anyone. It was never meant to be all that pleasant or all that nice.

Nasty Rock 'n' Roll

Now, I still like the music of the Sex Pistols. This might be a somewhat middle-aged thing to confess, but there is something in the album, *Never Mind the Bollocks, Here's the Sex Pistols,* that still makes it worth listening to. It's a perennially raw piece of music, and it still manages to sound aggressive and disagreeable. When Johnny Rotten wails: "Don't know what I want but / I know how to get it / I wanna destroy the passerby / 'Cos I-i-i wanna be-e — Anarchy!" – you know that he doesn't care whether we like it or not, and you assume that he'd prefer if we didn't. The Sex Pistols stood for many things, but being nice wasn't one of them.

In fact, the Sex Pistols was a consciously manufactured product, engineered to make people angry and outraged, and the story of the band is one of systematically seeking to be as unpleasant as possible. To a great degree this can be traced back to the band's manager, Malcolm McLaren (who seems to have been a very unpleasant man, and thus obviously one of my heroes), who realized that fitting in was not a good long-term strategy. He pioneered a marketing strategy that built on testing things, finding where the most vigorous resistance could be found, and then assaulting that full on. And, if possible, spit in someone's face in the process.

With this in mind, ask yourself: are the generally pleasant and positive feelings that surround the contemporary creativity discussion a good thing? Why are we so attracted to it, and what does this attraction do to the concept? And why is it that one so very, very seldom questions this family-friendly kind of creativity, sanitized for your consumption?

Right now, there are hundreds of creativity workshops going on, all over the world (but more prevalent in the Western world, particularly Europe and the US). Most, if not all, of these events are characterized by a general sense of pleasant, comfortable togetherness, and even the bad ones are characterized more by boredom than anyone becoming offended. Barring church services, a creativity workshop is the one place where you can count on getting an uplifting message and a sense of comfort in numbers.

Yes, the feeling that everyone can be creative and that creativity is fun-fun-fun is pleasant. Yes, it can give you that warm, fuzzy feeling inside when you're being spoon-fed a series of fun ideas and taught little creativity tricks. But is this feeling productive? Does truly creative work feel this harmonious, this *nice?* The answer is, that it doesn't. Does it help anyone? Maybe, on some psychological level, but probably not as much as people think it does. The risk, the real risk, is that all this lovely chit-chat might in fact mask a highly unproductive habit. This kind of creativity has, instead, become a way to avoid other discussions: you know, discussing those matters that aren't quite as nice as the bland and vacuum-packed happy pills so commonly doled out in the name of creativity.

Let's Not Talk About It

What creativity is supposed to do is help us humans live to our full potential; but this cannot be achieved by only looking at the things that we think are nice, or fun or suitable. No, creativity is all about reaching further, reaching beyond. In the same way that you can't become a top athlete (or even fit) if you choose only to exercise when it feels nice, you can't truly explore your creative potential if you stick to the things that seem easy and pleasant.

> What creativity is supposed to do is help us humans live to our full potential; but this cannot be achieved by only looking at the things that we think are nice, or fun or suitable. No, creativity is all about reaching further, reaching beyond.

So our first attack on the internal secret box will focus on facing the unpleasant and taking it seriously. So instead of asking what new ideas we could generate, in the best of all possible worlds, we could instead turn the issue on its head. What issues *don't* we want to talk about, what points are we *unwilling* to put on the agenda for the conference, what is it we *don't* want to cover when the theme is set as, "How can we become more creative in Company X?" Intriguing… What creativities might be out there, ignored and neglected because darn it, they're just not nice enough?

Crime and Punishment

Consider the fact that we could talk about criminal creativity, for such a thing obviously exists. But you already knew this, right? I'm guessing you're saying "Yeah, of course!" as you've seen the movies, *Ocean's Eleven*, *Twelve* and *Thirteen*. But do you really understand? Sure, all of us can talk the talk about how a burglar or a tax evader or a murderer can be creative, but does this mean that we're registering this when we talk about creativity? Are we using this as input when we try to extend our own creativity? On some analytical-rational level we obviously see this kind of **malevolent creativity** as real, but we are still much more prone to engage with the nicer forms, the more pleasant examples.

Why is this? We limit our discussions for many reasons. One is that we want be perceived as legitimate, serious individuals. We don't want people to question our motives, or our interests, so we tone down those parts of our thinking that we're not entirely sure that people will approve of. School is, of course, one of the main institutions where the killing of alternative creativities is part of the program. During our time in a company, we learn not to offend people or seem frivolous. After a while, this starts to become second nature to us – we subconsciously cut off those thoughts that we don't think are nice enough for public consumption. The real enemy of creativity isn't the boss or the school teachers: it's us.

But what would happen if we didn't do this, didn't just stick to the nice examples? Could we, for instance, learn something about creativity by studying torture? I can assure you that this is an issue that has never, ever been raised at the corporate creativity retreat – even if they can sometimes feel like torture. Still, if you were to see the manifold different ways in which totalitarian states abuse dissidents in their prisons, you can undoubtedly see a remarkable degree of inventive thinking, just as you could in the cases where very smart lawyers argued for tortu… I mean "harsh interrogation techniques", as being OK for the CIA to use. Sure, in cases of torture you can see an incredible evil, and a despicable disregard for humanity and human rights, but still…

Just the number of different ways in which clever (if probably sociopathic) people have been able to utilize electricity in order to inflict pain on other humans is nothing but astonishing, not to mention the huge number of less technological methods of torture. Just today, I was reading about the east African country of Eritrea, in which it seems that one method of punishment involves putting a person in a radial truck tyre and then beating the tyre (and the person being tortured) with clubs. Here the beating, the uncomfortable position, the vibrations from the tyre and the discomfort of being tightly enclosed add up to an almost unthinkable agony.

Unpleasant to think about? Definitively, but creative nonetheless. Please note that I'm not in any way trying to excuse or trivialize torture. The fact is, the very notion of creative torture makes me quite uncomfortable and even makes me shudder and recoil. It is this reaction that fascinates me. I've spent many years training myself to see creativity where others don't, to detect the creative impulse where others would not even look. Still, I find it exceptionally difficult to call a new method of torture creative, for there is something in the very inhumanity, the nastiness of it all, that almost physically forces me away from using the term "creativity" to describe it – and I'm supposed to be an expert!

There is something in our very thinking that restricts us from discussing the creativity of, for example, torture. Maybe this is a good thing. But if we are to be serious about it, and strictly analytical in our assessment, there is no rule that says a torturer cannot be creative. I've read studies of punishments and interrogation methods that in all their brutality are fantastic in their bestial inventiveness, even though I don't want to detail them further here – let it just be said that my example above is not the worst one by far that I've come across, not by far. Not calling these actions creative might seem like good manners – some things shouldn't really be discussed in polite company – but at the same time this habit of not talking about things that one feels uncomfortable with is one of the most efficient ways in which the discussion about creativity has become domesticated and flattened into a caricature of itself.

Creative Discomfort

If we were to look at companies, and the discussions within them, we can see some comparisons. We turn a blind eye to torture, as it is so deplorable and so deeply unethical, but at the same time there are many things in corporate life that we want to turn a blind eye to, as well. Even though these things cannot really live up to the depravity of the act of torture, there are many things that happen in a company that are so unpleasant, so difficult to engage with, that we simply discount them as unimportant. It might be an issue of the company being populated with only white, middle-aged, heterosexual, middle-class men, with creative diversity being something that other companies do. It might be an issue of our competitors having developed their business models in a way that makes us doubt that our current strategy has legs. Or it might be an issue of how the company is led, or even whether the company should be led at all.

Sure, these issues might be far removed from the evil that is torture by electric shock or beating, but they all represent issues that could be taboos in an organization, things that one just doesn't want to talk about. Let me give you an example. In my work as a sometime consultant, I once worked with a company with a business in technical services. In this example, the thing no one wanted to talk about, their specific ***point of creative discomfort,*** was the issue of "know-how".

Pain and Taboo

Points of discomfort are the places where we normally give in, stop stretching ourselves, since pain is a signal that the body (and mind) is protesting against a specific form of exertion in order to protect itself. If you're working with your body, you should take this seriously, and not try to force your muscles too far beyond the point that could cause strain and damage. Thinking, however, is a different matter. While the body can be damaged by going beyond its physical limitations, the mind is a much more resilient and elastic thing. We rarely capitalize upon this, rarely try to push our minds beyond their comfort zones to see what could be achieved. In the comfort zone things are simple, self-evident, assured; even holy.

Returning to my story, in the company we shall call Sordin,* the concept of know-how was one that everyone was supremely comfortable with. You might even say that this was their holiest of holies. When they talked about themselves, this was what they highlighted. This was also the one thing that was written into every vision they'd formulated, every strategy they'd brought forth, every formulation of their values they had ever developed. Each and every time the company started internal (or external) discussions about innovation, developing new ideas or strategy, the emphasis on know-how was reinforced again and again. We might even say that this had become their religion, their mantra.

So, me being me, this was the first thing I started working on when I ran a seminar on creativity for their top management. I asked the gathered executives to develop a novel strategy for

---

* Which was in reality called something completely different. Thanks, non-disclosure contract!

the corporation, but added that this had to build upon the notion that the company did not have any know-how of its own, and that all forms of expertise had to be outsourced. All of a sudden, the exercise, which was supposed to be quite easy, and one they'd gone through a number of times before, became exceptionally difficult. Quite a few of the top-ranking managers started fidgeting, while others started muttering and otherwise signaling their displeasure and discomfort. This continued for a short while, until one of them decided that he'd had enough and bellowed: "But this is nonsense! What's the point of ideating about a situation where our best and only competitive advantage is gone?" Which, obviously, was the point.

What does this imply? In short: if an organization or an individual wants to become more creative and better at developing new ideas, one needs to start by asking what kinds of ideas are seen as forbidden, unsuitable, stupid or difficult to talk about. In other words, developing serious creativity is a question of *facing the taboos of creativity*. In the same way as we shudder at the thought of creatively applied torture, the executives at Sordin Inc. shied away from the creative space that was made when the assumptions about their world-leading know-how were removed.

Examining malevolent expressions of creativity can be a way of combating the tendency to ignore or distance oneself from things that do not seem proper and nice to think about. Thinking about malevolent creativity can be a kind of shock therapy for the brain, a way of forcing it out of its comfort zone. But it is only one approach, and we'll consider many others. In this first stage of exploring dangerous thinking the key point to grasp is that it is precisely when things start being a little less pleasant, at the moment when executives start fidgeting, that the seriously creative starts to make itself known.

> It is precisely when things start being a little less pleasant, at the moment when executives start fidgeting, that the seriously creative starts to make itself known.

Embracing Discomfort

Recognizing this insight allows discomfort to find a place in the discussion. Each organization and each individual have their own points of discomfort and pain, so it is necessary to begin by identifying the existing norms that hinder creativity. These norms take many shapes and guide great swaths of our thinking – they decide what we see as important, nice, beautiful, effective, *et cetera,* and they guide our actions and decision-making.

Having ascertained this, the next step is to mercilessly and aggressively attack them. When the Sex Pistols were about to seriously launch their only real album, Malcolm McLaren, the band's manager, ensured the group utilized even Queen Elizabeth's 1977 Silver Jubilee with the single, "God Save the Queen", as a particularly egregious provocation. The band chartered a boat to defiantly play this little piece of norm(ality) breaking music from the River Thames, in front of both the Houses of Parliament and Westminster, but were stopped by the police and forced to bring the performance to a close. Put somewhat differently, McLaren was highly attuned to the points of discomfort in the collective psyche of the British establishment, and used this insight to see how far he could push things. Society reacted, strongly, and his creative project was an immediate success. This is why the Sex Pistols still live on in our collective consciousness.

Exploring such points of discomfort is, of course, not a simple thing. It isn't easy in organizations, where it will by logical necessity create a lot of resistance, and it isn't easy when it comes to your own thinking, as this means you need to face a lot of uncomfortable things about yourself. But it can be done, if you work at it.

A first step in this development is to list the five things you believe are crucial in your work or your company, and then try to engage with their complete antitheses. If the corporation thinks that it is important to work more closely with the customer and focus on the technology, it is, in all likelihood, much more productive to sometimes ignore this and focus on design instead – at least for a while. Another approach is to analyze which ideas are first ignored when working with a corporation's strategic development, and use this as a roadmap to plotting which assumptions are guiding the organization's thinking – and what could be a really creative way out of it. For what are the ideas that are so uncomfortable, so punk, that they need to be swiftly ignored? And which are the ideas of norms and normality that guide you, that create your roadmap to bland, safe thinking?

An Uncomfortable Truth

Pause here for a while. Make a list of the kinds of thoughts and ideas that you, without really thinking about it, instinctively feel won't work or won't fit in your organization. Which are the things you don't want brought up at meetings, the things that make you mad? Now start looking at this collection of irritations. Ask yourself: "How would I act if I knew that this is where the biggest potential to develop and improve me and my company lies?" You may have struggled with creating a list, which goes to show just how difficult it is to look beyond that which makes us feel safe and comfortable. You might feel that these are not the things that make you engaged and fired up. This latter point is important. We are naturally inclined to follow that which engages and inspires us, but this comes at a price. Being inspired by something is in part a sensation of recognition, of being comfortable doing something – inspiration stems from cognitive fluency. And this comfort is, as already stated, dangerous. What might seem like creativity could in fact be *conservative thinking in fancy dress.*

For corporations that want to become more creative, this is even more of a trap. If a new strategy feels really, really inspiring, it's probably a load of crap. Inspiration and passion are things we are instinctively drawn to, things we are hardwired to like. The problem is that there is something hidden in these good vibrations. The brain, that wily organ, just happens to be amazingly good at generating a feeling of inspiration and passion *specifically* in order to make us focus on thing we already know and are comfortable with, rather than forcing us into those uncomfortable spheres where we can start challenging our thinking. Inspiration can at times be a way for the brain to disguise the comfortable and the well-known, a way to create a haze that makes

If a new strategy feels really, really inspiring, it's probably a load of crap.

us see our most conservative forms of thinking **Inspiration, passion and pleasure** as creative and novel – habitual thinking doped **can be a smokescreen!** up on dopamine fumes. This is the reason why organizations so often cheerfully run through the same processes of change time after time, and even manage to feel inspired in doing so. This is also why we can come up with the same idea time and time again, and still feel as if it's as fresh and new. *Inspiration, passion and pleasure can be a smokescreen!*

But how are we to encounter the uncomfortable, and how can we recognize it? First and foremost, by pulling away. The big problem with becoming more creative is that it involves rigorously going against one's mental conditioning, of *not going towards that which feels instinctively right.* Malcolm Gladwell's book, *Blink,* popularized the notion of going with your gut, which is great in situations where you can be sure that your old thinking applies, but devastating in situations where what you're trained to appreciate no longer applies – a lesson many companies have learnt the hard way.

Gut feelings are the enemy of creativity! To state that there is an anti-creativity bias in *Blink* might sound a tad brutal. Still, if you are more interested in developing new thinking rather **Gut feelings are the enemy** than becoming very good at utilizing what you **of creativity!** already know, you need to face the fact that your instinct is primed to take you into your comfort zone, i.e., into a zone where creativity is mainly absent. See, creativity isn't necessarily supposed to be all that fun! On the contrary, if it feels fun, there's a risk. Sure, it can be fun *as well,* but if you feel quite at home in the process of "creating", part of what is happening is that your brain is tricking you. *Again.*

Your First Questions Suck

Some might see this as just another way of saying, "You should question everything!" – a cheerful exhortation you can find in most books on creativity. But it isn't. *Questioning everything is just stupid,* since it is often yet another version of doing that which one is conditioned to do – asking the questions that come most comfortably to you – and a part of the brain's lazy habit of seeking the most comfortable position.

To get further than this, try questioning three things about your company: for example, your company's strategy, or the way in which you go about your work or whatever other activity you want to question. Go ahead, I'll wait. This is the first step, and it is well-known and quite easy to do. The important step, however, is the next one. What are you going to do with these three questions? Pat yourself on the back for being such a free-thinking individual? Sure, if that's what makes you feel good. Hasn't got anything to do with creativity, but still. The important step, the one that you need to take if you want to break with conventional thinking, is to turn the issue around. Look at your three questions. Are you happy with them?

Look again, and this time consider why these were the first things you thought of. They are, in a sense, a perfect image not of how clever you are, but how limited your thinking is. The three questions are important, for they can be used to confront your conservatism face-to-face. Why these questions? And why did it feel so effortless to ask them? Look again at the questions, but start seeing them as meaningless; they are nothing but your brain's own special way of disguising its conservative and habitual bias. Study the questions, by all means, but realize that these aren't the fundamental ones: such fundamental questions lie hidden somewhere deep in the shadowlands beyond the confines of the secret box. In order to reach that deeper level, something more than mere questioning is needed. We need to dig deep, to shock and awe, to tear down veils.

We started this chapter with a tale from Tim Ferriss. Let's reconsider that. Did he ask the obvious question about kickboxing? No. Very consciously, he'd learnt not to look at the obvious questions, such as, "How can I kick harder?" or "Can I learn a better way of blocking?" Instead, he looked at the rules, and tried to find one that no one was utilizing, one that people accepted uncritically. Pushing people out of a ring was not a nice solution, and it caused considerable upset to purists of the sport. But it was an effective solution that started from an inquiry into what kinds of behaviours other participants couldn't imagine engaging in, and then doing just those things.

GET DISGUSTED — AND DISGUSTING

Almost anything that can be praised or advocated has been put to some disgusting use. There is no principle, however immaculate, that has not had its compromising manipulator.

—Wyndham Lewis

One of my all-time favourite products is a kind of candy, more specifically a kind of candy with very weird packaging. The product in question happens to be an ear made out of plastic, where the ear canal is plugged. This plug can be removed, and once you open it up, you can take the Q-tip that the makers were kind enough to supply you with and start eating the generous layers of wax you can find inside the ear. Fun, right? Obviously, the Q-tip isn't really a Q-tip, and the earwax is actually a very sweet candy sludge that children find delicious. I don't particularly like the candy, but I love the effect it has on people. When I lecture, and the time comes to show off this product, I only have to utter the magic words "…and then you eat the earwax…" in order to see how people shudder in their chairs, instinctively pulling back. If it is a bigger audience you can hear a distinct "Eeeewwww…" reverberating through the lecture hall. Fantastic. Eating earwax is utterly disgusting, and therefore, a great example of creative thinking.

What is fascinating about this kind of reaction and the associated feeling of disgust is that it can give us a special insight into how creativity works. Let's take a step back, to the moment where the disgust becomes manifest. Think about it, dear reader, and imagine that you're one of the people in the audience. I'm talking directly to you, saying, "…and then you're eating the earwax like this, yum, yum!" You consider it, and immediately regret it. You might even get a sensation as if you've tasted earwax, and that is not at all pleasant. You turn away a little, you frown, and the word "bleugh" goes through your head.

What is happening in this moment? At an earlier stage of your life, when you were a child, these kinds of reactions were a lot rarer. Back when you were a kid, you were interested in things such as what earwax, or snot, or even urine tasted like. You weren't that easy to shock back then, but something happened. You learnt that some things are suitable and good, and others disgusting and improper. At first, this was only a question of being told off by mum or dad, but later on you started to control and regulate yourself, and others. If you saw somebody picking their nose in class you yelled out, "Man, you're disgusting!" You'd learnt and absorbed what was suitable and what wasn't, and somewhere in that process your creativity died a little.

Think back to that moment of disgust. What you feel right then, the resistance that develops and which almost physically repels you, this is a pure form of your mind's limitations making themselves known. You might even say that this is the moment when you can actually feel the walls of the secret box. In the moment you feel disgust, it is as if a part of your brain is shut down. You're pushed away, and through this you lose access to parts of your mind's potential. The funny thing about this process is that your own mind makes this happen, that enacts this curtailing and separation. We could even say that it is your mind shutting itself down. The feeling of disgust is like a very limited lobotomy that the brain performs on itself, all in order to protect its sense of integrity and to preserve the borders of controlled thinking.

But that feeling of disgust has benefits: here, we can feel the limitations of our mind in a very tangible way. The resistance we feel presents itself to us as an almost physical barrier – and this might be the closest we can come to experiencing the secret box on a phenomenological level.

Something inside us creates a friction, pushes us away; being faced with disgust and similar sensations can almost feel like being blocked at a threshold, being barred from entering a place.

The Fat Duck

In the last chapter I talked about the attractions and pitfalls of pleasant feelings and thoughts. The disgusting is a very powerful example of that which is not pleasant, and thereby also an example of phenomena that do not fit in with the disguised conservatism of our everyday creativity. But the disgusting is also something more powerful, something that creates a discomfort and a sensation of having transgressed. We rarely get disgusted by ourselves, even when we're being disgusting, and instead our feelings of revulsion are normally a reaction to things outside us, things that feel invasive. The disgusting is, in a way, a strongly enhanced and more personal version of the unpleasant, and thus better as a pedagogical example when we try to explore the limits to our normal thinking.

Snail Porridge

We can consider another example: snail porridge. Taste those words – "snail porridge". Doesn't evoke pleasant thoughts, does it? Most people I talk to about this look disconcerted and insist we change the subject. This is especially if we happen to be eating a meal, since it sounds like something a child would dream up in order to gross out their parents or friends. Still, the fact is that not only does snail porridge exist, it is part of the tasting menu at *The Fat Duck* (in Bray, UK), one of the best restaurants in the world – three Michelin stars, and permanent pride of place at the top of world rankings. The chef and proprietor of this restaurant is that odd genius Heston Blumenthal, a man that has invested a lot of energy into not letting anything limit his view of food and its potential. For him, there is no such thing as a food that would be fundamentally disgusting, just food he hasn't tasted and cooked yet. His snail porridge is a brilliant example of this, and shows what you can achieve if you have faith in being able to create something interesting by combining something as classically French as snails with something so quintessentially British as oatmeal porridge.

A common way to describe creativity is to see it as the art of combining two already existing things into something novel and surprising. Snail porridge is a great example of this – two established foodstuffs combined into something eminently unique. Creativity research loves examples like this, but has had great difficulties in explaining why we embrace some things and not others. This is due to a basic fact in the way our brains' function.

In order to understand creativity we need to engage with two processes running in parallel. On one side, we have the process where we learn things, i.e., where we increase the amount of facts we know and that we can hypothetically combine. This is what one usually focuses on, partly because it is so easy to talk about all the ways in which you or your organization can stockpile facts and knowledge and so develop talent and increase capabilities. You can read more, travel more, talk to new people, try to manage for an entire day wearing a blindfold – it will all teach you something. Your organization can take trips to a jellybean factory (as the team designing the iMac did), hire artists or sushi chefs or clowns to shake up the talent pool, or just put an emphasis on diversity. There are many ways of stockpiling.

However, this is only one part of the process. The other side of it, the one that is trickier to control, is the one where all these fact, all this knowledge, all these talents, become classified by your mind as being either legitimate and OK to utilize; or illegitimate, disgusting, even dangerous. We are normally unaware of this limiting process, this *process of legitimization,* and it is this limiting process that we need to work with or against when we're trying to come to grips with the role of disgust in creativity.

The Brain as an Engine

You can become more creative just through learning more, this much is true on a trivial level. Still, what you're doing then is working with conceptual expansion, adding elements to a limited sphere of your thinking and its potential. By reflecting on what you see as legitimate material to utilize in thinking, and contrasting it with what you see as disgusting or dumb, you are instead working with making your mind more capable of utilizing all it knows. By re-evaluating the boundaries of legitimate thinking you're in effect increasing the value of what you already know.

As an illustration, think about buying a car. You can choose the features: a really big gas tank (i.e., can fit a lot of more of the same) or good gas mileage (i.e., the engine can utilize what it has more efficiently). The same goes for the way you approach thinking. You can keep working on increasing the amount of fuel you can carry, i.e., focusing on getting more information about more things, but this will rarely create very surprising results. If you instead focus on making the engine more efficient, i.e., work at being able to utilize all that you already know, you'll increase the possibility that you can generate something truly novel.

What the disgust response highlights is a kind of inefficiency in our thinking, a way in which we could tune our creative engine. This is also why disgust is important, for if we can face this specific limitation, it will become easier for us to see other ways in which we are unconsciously shunning things as not being legitimate topics in a discussion about creativity. When confronted with feelings of disgust we not only feel a slight irritation because things are not as comfortable as we would like them to be, but a very personal discomfort, a very personal way of shutting some things out. This closed door on our creativity is not just one that hinders us from outside, like a bureaucratic organization or a mean boss, but a personal impediment we're carrying around and taking as given.

> What the disgust response highlights is a kind of inefficiency in our thinking, a way in which we could tune our creative engine.

Selling – How Disgusting!

So, one path on the way to creativity is to face the different ways in which your mind limits itself by categorizing things as disgusting, or offensive, or discomforting. As an example (one less disgusting that the others but just as telling), we could take the simple fact that a lot of people find selling things, i.e., pushing other people to buy from them, quite disagreeable. While the corporate world is screaming out for good salesmen (and creativity in selling, a massively important area), people entering the corporate world mostly dream about other things. I see this in a particularly harsh light when I work with teaching the art of new business ideas. Almost 100 per cent (there's that figure again) of the business plans or drafts presented to me focus solely on the product, and maybe a little on the fun strategy work. That someone needs to do the grunt work of selling, really going out there to schlep a sales kit around, this is mostly ignored. When I ask about this curious fact, I always encounter the same answer: "We'll hire salespeople!"

What this means is that more or less all of the business plans that I've come across (and it's a considerable number at this point) are handicapped by their authors who, just like the rest of us, have a tendency not to really engage with things that they feel uncomfortable about. Taken a little further, this means that almost every business plan I've seen has been less creative than it could be, for the simple reason that they haven't utilized the possibilities that exist outside of their comfort zones. If we find selling repulsive, we'll shy away from it, even if it is the most important thing for our business. Our rational mind can quite often lead us to irrational positions.

Revolting Machines

Another thing people normally find uncomfortable is high-heeled shoes. And something most men find positively disgusting is dressing up in women's clothing ("What will other men think?"). This is why in 2007, General Motors ran a project in which car designers and engineers had to do exactly that. By trying to get in and out of GM's cars in dresses and high heels, these (almost all male) engineers could learn a lot about their female customers, but maybe even more about themselves. Dressing up as a woman was uncomfortable and a little icky, and it was precisely because of this that it could generate new insights. Rather than just brainstorming, the change in perspective could challenge the creative norms in the organization, highlighting the kinds of solutions that were truly creative as opposed to those that were merely lazy. Yes, it might have been a case of too little, too late, but there's still much to learn from experiments such as these.

We began this book by discussing the Flip Video, the basic video camera that threatened the more established models. We could easily have taken another example – the advent of the netbook. Small, cheap, relatively slow laptops proved to be a runaway success for the medium-sized companies that brought them to market. Again, the same question arises: why wasn't it one of the established major corporations that introduced this new type of product? The answer: for the same reason that the Flip Video was created by a company no one had ever heard of. There are many similarities between the two cases. Both were distinctly different ideas in their context, but they were also provocative, disturbing notions for those already in that business. An engineer who works with developing laptops is normally obsessed with the idea of technical excellence. Generally speaking, engineers tend to subscribe to a macho ethos of "more is better" – bigger screens, faster processors, more bang for your buck. The machine becomes a symbol of the engineer's virility, power and competence. To do something worse, something less powerful – that's just repulsive.

In the IT business, people saw netbooks as provocative, and not in a positive way. Cheap crap, not to put too fine a word on it. Nothing a serious person would want to engage with. Disgusting, ridiculous and stupid. But successful, oh so successful… IKEA is a similar example. When they introduced their radical notion of buying furniture in flat packs that required assembly, the furniture industry turned up their noses. It was just unseemly – cheap trash you had to build yourself? How could anyone be proud of such a product? History has, of course, shown that there was much to be proud of in this, but still, many people were appalled.

What disgusts you?

What would disgust others in your business?

What dangerous thinking demands of us is that we go beyond this instinctive reaction of disgust and push beyond our cognitive fluency. In every business, there are things that one is proud of, things that are seen as conventionally praiseworthy. Those who can go beyond this create revolutions.

Geriatric Porn

To take an example that's going to be a reality for all of us sooner or later, think about being elderly. We live in a world which is turning ever more grey, a world where people who are 60 years old or above are increasing and becoming more important. Still, this group is habitually ignored when we think and talk about creativity and new ideas. To take one of my favourite examples (and touch upon the theme of the next chapter), how often do you, for instance, think about sex between the elderly? Unless you are of a somewhat more advanced age yourself, the likelihood is that you don't, really. And if you are, you're thinking about it *a lot,* much more than people realize… Herein lies a possibility and an illustration.

In my circle of acquaintances there are a number of women who are aged 60 plus, lovely and wonderful people who I care about a lot. Some of them are single, and I guess you can see where I'm going with this. It is a simple, almost trivial fact that there is a huge group of singles that are over the age of 60, and a great part of this group does not want to become sexually inactive. Regardless of this, there is a lack of entrepreneurs involved in "dating for the elderly" businesses, and we have a catastrophic lack of ideas when it comes to reshaping social life for a world where a growing cadre of senior citizens are becoming hipper, healthier and hornier. We have Viagra and then… nothing. Why? Because for those of us who aren't elderly, the thought of geriatric fornication is a bit disgusting, and we really don't want to think about it. A massive consumer group, a well-defined need, a clear social demand – and no ideas. No amount of nice young men talking about how lovely creativity is can help us here.

The world is filled with strange things, and we all carry around certain prejudices. Maybe you get irritated by kids wearing their jeans really low on their hips, or get nervous in a bus filled with people whose ethnicity does not match yours. Some find football fans disconcerting, while others get nauseous when subjected to country music (incredible, I know, but the world is a strange place). All these reactions are caused by your brain's switches and barriers when dealing with the disgusting and the scary, and these all work in concert to limit and hamper your creativity. Yes, you can keep doing only those things that make you feel happy and pleased and comfortable, and yes, such well-being is good and important. But it's not necessarily the best thing for your thinking, and definitively not for your creativity.

Make a List

Therefore, if you want to make you creative engine more efficient, list the 20 things you like the least. Make this list as honest as you can, a private and secret list, and include all the things you might not normally admit to disliking or finding discomforting. You might be slightly xenophobic and afraid of Muslims, so list that. You might find gay men objectionable. You might hate dogs, or kittens or children. List those things. The list exists only for your own perusal, and can be burnt after reading. The important point is to be honest about the number of things you do not like, the things you don't want to think about; and then realize that each and every one of these things represents a way in which you've made yourself less creative than you could be, less free in your thinking, and thereby radically diminished in your potential to enact change in the world.

Don't misunderstand me here: the point is not learning to love everything, for that is simply not possible. We all have dislikes, subtle or not so subtle prejudices that affect our thinking. Eradicating them completely is impossible, for they are a part of us. The important thing to understand is that working with your creativity needs to be about facing up to these things and taking them seriously. You have to realize that your mind has these barriers, things that cannot be shifted by the normal games and exercises creativity coaches so happily throw at you. There is so much more going on in our minds, and so much more to discover about our world, if we are willing to accept things as they are rather than letting fixed notions of legitimacy limit us. For as strange as it may sound, you can become a lot more creative by becoming a little more disgusting.

OBSCENE THINKING, YAY!

It is good taste, and good taste alone, that possesses the power to sterilize and is always the first handicap to any creative functioning.

—Salvador Dali

The creative process is a cocktail of instinct, skill, culture and a highly creative feverishness. It is not like a drug; it is a particular state when everything happens very quickly, a mixture of consciousness and unconsciousness, of fear and pleasure; it's a little like making love, the physical act of love.

—Francis Bacon

I have an image on my laptop that encapsulates a lot of my take on creativity, and I just love to use it when I lecture on the subject. It is a picture of something so mundane as a hair colouring product, where the only original aspect is that the colour in question is pink. Well, maybe not the only original thing, as the colouring happens to have been specially developed to be used for pubic hair. Yep, if you want your genitals to be framed in a lovely shade of pink, this is now completely possible! A forward-looking entrepreneur by the name of Nancy Jarecki realized that some women (and in all likelihood a few men as well) obviously coloured their hair, and that when they did so, they might be interested in matching the carpet to the drapes. However, the normal colouring agents use chemicals that are too strong for the more sensitive pubic area, so Nancy developed a series called *Betty*; the pink colour I have a picture of is called *Fun Betty*.

The reason I use this image is not due to some particular interest in pubic hair, but because of the response I tend to get. What usually happens is that people first look up in a confused manner, then shy away just the tiniest bit and lastly start to giggle nervously. For some mysterious reason it doesn't seem as common as you'd think for a management professor to talk about and display images of pubic hair – amazingly enough! Or, to be a little more precise, to show an image of a package that timidly shows a coloured triangle somewhere in the pelvic region of a stylized image of a woman's body.

In much the same way as my earlier example of candy in the form of earwax gave people little ticks of disgust, so the image of pink pubic hairs tends to create a small shock-effect in an audience, a feeling that originates from how the brain, in an almost physically tangible way, tries to kick out an improper idea. The brain knows full well that sex, or things that are close to thoughts about sex, are not things to be openly pondered, particularly not when we're meant to be considering something as serious as creativity (and looking at some of the people in the creativity business, this decision seems quite natural – I'd rather not think of these people having sex either). The brain knows that sex is obscene, sinful and downright filthy. Particularly when it is good sex. ("Ba-da-boom! Thank you, ladies and gentlemen, I'll be here all week! Tip your waitresses, and please try the fish.")

In *exactly* the same way as the brain will shut out the things it feels are disgusting, it will shun the things it feels are indecent and dirty. All these things exist in the area outside of your secret box, the box that controls and limits our thinking, and which cannot be shifted without a serious attack on the feelings of propriety that secretly keep us locked to specific patterns of thinking. The dirty is different from the disgusting, for where the latter is related to what creates a sense of repulsion, the former is a question about what is seen as improper. When we say that something is obscene and indecent, we're saying that these are things that shouldn't be brought out into the open, things that are not discussed in polite company. The disgusting is connected to breaking with good manners, but the obscene is an issue of breaking much more fundamental taboos. Lucky for us, creativity should be about breaking taboos.

Luckily, there is a much deeper connection between creativity and sex. Sex is a primal drive, and an exceptionally important and fundamental one. Many of the people who have dabbled in creative activities – by playing in a band, developing an interest in theatre or art, or just liking creativity workshops – have done this for a simple reason. They hope it'll help them to get laid. And science supports this viewpoint! In their brilliant article, "Schizotypy, creativity and mating success in humans" (published in 2006 in *Procedures of Biological Science,* volume 273), D. Nettle & H. Clegg focus on the one critical issue regarding creativity: "Do creative people get laid more often than others?" Lo and behold, the answer is a heartfelt "Yes!" If this doesn't convince you about the importance of this book, you and I have nothing to talk about. But I'm pretty sure I know how your mind works, and I do think I know what you like – you can stop acting all coy. So let's get a little obscene, shall we?

Will You Be Queer Zero?

Here's an example, to kick us off: why did it take so damn long for the cosmetics industry to launch high-end skincare products for men? Not that long ago the products available to men were generic unisex products, without clear branding. Now, the niche of grooming products for men is booming, and it is obvious that the market is there. But why did it take so long? Some would argue that this is due to men not being prepared to buy them until recently, and that the products turned up when the demand was there. Right. Suuuure…

No, consumption does not work like this. No one wrote angry letters to L'Oréal to complain about their lack of products for men, and no one walked around dreaming of the day they could spend some serious money on a cream that included Daily Extreme Moisture Defence

Formula. Instead, men (and sometimes their partners) discovered that the products were out there and immediately started buying them in cartloads, as soon as the corporations started putting them on the shelves. So what was the corporation's problem?

To my mind, the problem is obvious. The issue wasn't that there was a lack of the more limited kind of creativity, but that in order to make a radical innovation like this, companies needed to enact a very special kind of change in the boardroom. I call this *the principle of Queer Zero* (not unlike that of Patient Zero in a pandemic outbreak). Queer does not here refer to a sexual orientation, but to the notion of being different, of not like the others. Often, nobody wants to be the first queer one out there, the first person who breaks with the norm. No one wants to be the first to challenge the way in which the organization one works in constructs its identity and self-image. We want to be seen as "normal", as "just like the others", and are exceedingly afraid of looking like a freak. Not to mention looking queer.

Books on creativity habitually comment upon the uncertainty that accompanies new ideas, but note that analyses tend to focus solely on the fear of being criticized. This is a dangerously limited outlook. Sure, such fears are very real, but represent just a superficial phenomenon if we want to understand how creativity is held back. Even though there is a kind of uneasiness in connection with wondering whether people will think your new idea is bad, this is a minor issue compared with the fear of being "queer" or a "freak". In the former case, the worst that can happen is that people think you're a tad stupid, whereas it is your very identity that is questioned in the latter. Returning to the office after having said something stupid at a meeting isn't all that difficult, but if your idea has challenged accepted norms and identities, you might very quickly find that you've been defined by this one norm(ality) breaking incident.

In the case of moisturizers for men, no one wanted to be the person who broke with the conventional view that men are all tough, hard, massively heterosexual guys, full of piss and vinegar, all of whom would rather die than do something as sissy as using skincare products. The tiny little detail that men are massively vain, and prepared to pay almost any sum in order to keep believing that they are still good-looking and capable of seducing 20-year-old supermodels (something I obviously could do, seeing as I use a restoring serum containing essential minerals – or at least that's what I'd like to think), this was conveniently ignored. After all, one didn't want to seem queer.

Rainbow Kindergarten

Consider the following: in highly liberal Sweden, it is estimated that there are approximately 40,000 children who live in so-called "rainbow families", i.e., families with same-sex parents. Estimates regarding rainbow families in the United States are difficult to come by, but assuming that the rates in the US would be as low as 25 per cent of the Swedish levels, it would still mean some 340,000 children living in rainbow families. In Sweden, up to 2007, there was not a single daycare centre or kindergarten that was designed to provide a service for this group. Let's review this: on one side there's a huge consumer group, on the other, *not a single entrepreneur developing services for it.*

Now, obviously not all gay families want a special kindergarten, nor should all entrepreneurs focus on this group. The main reason I'm focusing on this group is to highlight that our search for things such as market opportunities might be affected by biases we're not even aware of. In the same way as the brain shuts out things it feels are unpleasant, we often, quite automatically and unconsciously, ignore things that our culture and upbringing has taught us are improper to talk about. All things sexual belong to this sphere, but it seems that homosexuality is a particularly deep-rooted taboo, an exceptionally tough barrier to creative thinking. So things that are even close to this, or that through different preconceived notions can be connected to this, automatically becomes "somebody else's business" – and in some cases a very successful business indeed.

Desire, Desire!

On a fundamental level this is a question of *desire,* and our incapacity to talk and think about the role of desire in society. Desire is not proper, not appropriate, at least not in the way we implicitly assume that "efficiency" or "needs" are. Still, the fact is that for most of our lives, almost all of it in fact, we are controlled by desire. We are continuously affected by wanting things we might not need but still yearn for. Professor Micael Dahlén, an expert in consumer behaviour, has called our current way of living "the expectation society". In a book entitled *Nextopia,* he argues that we are generally more driven by wanting the next thing than the actual act of consuming things, and he may be on to something. Society is to a great extent built upon desire, and real desire is never fulfilled.

But this is difficult to own up to in a society that insists upon certain forms of behaviour if you're to be taken seriously as a person. We're expected to give rational explanations for our behaviours, deny our desires, or at least disguise them as something much more rationally driven than they are. This is also why we are so blind towards the desires of others, or openly denigrate them. We live in *a moral society,* and we try to ignore or marginalize everything that does not fit into our moral framework. So we do not want to recognize the significance of sexuality, or other ways of living, or even our own desires. And this negatively affects our creativity.

Morality is one of the most powerful weapons that the brain has at its disposal for protecting the secret box. We might even say that this is our brain's primary way of controlling us, of seeing to it that we do not walk outside the parameters of legitimate thought. Our moral sense turns up in different guises: "We really shouldn't be doing things like this," or "Can't we try to be a little serious now?" or "Management wouldn't like that," or "Are we supposed to stoop to this?" and the more concise, "Eww!" Our moralization of issues ties us to the things that are proper, the things everyone can accept, the bland and the middle-of-the-road. Moralization keeps us tied to the things that do not irritate people. Succinctly put, morality keeps us stuck in the non-creative.

So to break with this, to bring some of that dirty thing called creativity into the equation, you might have to get a little obscene in your thinking. Obviously I'm not saying that you should have orgies in your meeting room – regardless of how fun that might be, depending on how freaky your colleagues are – but that you need to push your thinking into the realm of desire, beyond the barriers of the proper. This is a case of accepting that our creative role, particularly if we're doing so in the framework of a company, is not to tell people how they should live their lives but instead enable them to do things, realize their potential, and achieve their desires.*

We're All Sinners

Here is an example from the service industry: I'm not a morning person, and I often stay at hotels for my work. Why is it that so many hotels put away the breakfast buffet at 10 a.m. sharp? Even though I've often paid an exorbitant amount for my room, I have to accept that if I want to eat breakfast, I have to eat it at the "proper" time, regardless. I happen to like a nice, big breakfast at around 11 a.m., if possible, but for some reason hotels seem to find this highly improper, and an indication that I'm an immoral person (they might be right, but that's really none of their business). So they do a lot of work to see to it that I either conform or get punished. Obviously the hotel is looking out for my soul, wanting to ensure that I don't do something as unseemly as sleep late or have sex during daylight hours, and do what they can to control me, even by deciding when I can eat my breakfast – our sins have to be punished.

A surprising number of companies in the service industry work according to similar principles. You (that is the customer) are supposed to behave in a conventional way. You're supposed to plan things ahead of time. You're supposed to do things during business hours. You're supposed to take out money in advance. You're not supposed to think that things can be done in a different way. The connection to sex might seem tenuous, but the underlying principle is the same – to ensure that people behave "properly". Men are not supposed to use cosmetics. Customers should understand how we do things around here. People who want a drink alcohol on the early London-Copenhagen flight are not the kind of people we want as customers. And so it goes.

---

* Within certain limits, obviously - corporations shouldn't support criminal or destructive behaviours. And corporations should try to be ethical in all they do. But should they strive for morality? That's the question...

If you want to develop a more creative organization, one step towards this is to accept that people have different desires, different ways to approach things, and it isn't the role of the organization to define which of these are "proper", for if you let yourself be limited by the things that are "proper" you will not get as far as you otherwise could. I started this chapter with a slightly smutty example, which when observed a little more closely wasn't very smutty at all. Most people who'll read this book have pubic hair, and there is nothing dirty about it. To colour this might seem like an odd thing to do, but if that's something that you want to do, why not?

The interesting thing to consider here is not why people would like to do so, but why we react uncomfortably to the example. Did it confuse you? Did you blush? Did you think the example was silly, or uninteresting, or juvenile? All these reactions spring from ways in which your brain is trying to keep you in check and ensure that your thoughts do not veer into forbidden, unsuitable areas. And it is up to you to decide whether it is you who are in charge when it comes to deciding what to think, or if your super-ego, your moral conscience, should continue to hold the reins.

TO HELL WITH ADULTHOOD

Children begin by loving their parents; as they grow older they judge them; sometimes, they forgive them.

—Oscar Wilde

Every child is an artist. The problem is how to remain an artist once we grow up.

—Pablo Picasso

Irrespective of what you think of kids, you can't accuse them of being overly sophisticated. They enjoy discussing bodily waste, they laugh at farts, and have no issue with walking around with snot all over their face. This is also why they are innovative, creative and inquisitive. As nature's own punk rockers they are gloriously free from conventions, and if there is the possibility of challenging these norms, they are almost frighteningly acute in their capacity to find ways to do so. Yes, we all know that children are creative, yet we seldom pause to ask exactly what it is that makes them so. Instead, we prefer to romanticize the issue, and view kids endeavours through rose-tinted glasses. But the creativity of children is not just something cute and lovely, but an unfettered, anarchic impulse that we later spend an enormous amount of energy inhibiting in ourselves. Strange, but true – and toxic for creative development.

Children are egoistic, unsophisticated and greedy little creatures (and this goes for my two little rays of sunshine, as well). Their redeeming quality, however, is that they are completely shameless about this, and delightfully open with their foibles. If a child wants a cookie, he or she won't present a series of excuses to have it, such as that they feel stressed and need to relax, or that they want to test how the cookie would taste with their juice. Instead, they just want the damn cookie. If the child likes a silly TV series without any aesthetic or cultural value, the child couldn't care less about justifying this liking. Niceties are mostly lost on children. Where adults are programmed to explain away their passions and vices with a series of excuses ("–It's not that I *like* reality TV, but sometimes I think it is interesting to watch it as a way to understand the minds of the rabble…"), children are OK with liking any number of silly things without excuse.

And although we're loath to say it, we're more like kids than we want to admit. Even though we are conditioned to deny it, the fact is that we all love silly things, stupid things, toys and frippery. Sure, we've become really good at hiding this impulse by calling it something else, and we are not happy with our beloved expenditures being called by these (real) names, but the fact still stands. Take home decoration, for instance. No person in their right mind can claim that the enormous amount of money being poured in to designed vases and luxurious materials is strictly functional, or that it would be a life-or-death matter whether one gets a new kitchen or an Italian designer sofa. No, these are childish things, unneeded things, frivolities. Your beloved home theatre system is just a different variety of a Barbie or G.I. Joe, just as unnecessary and as silly. *But it's OK!* There is no reason to say that our love of the unnecessary, the showy or the frivolous is a problem or a weakness; quite the contrary.

The Necessity of Frivolity

If we, as humans, only consumed what we truly needed to survive, every single aspect of the global economy would crash, more or less immediately. With the exception of some of the most destitute people on earth, most consumption, even in the poorer countries, is in fact a function of humanity's desire for the extraneous. Tribes in the Andes spend what little they have on colourful clothing, and tribes in the jungles of Borneo spend a surprising amount of their time adorning their homes and creating artifacts for ritual use. We in the West obviously spend on a much greater scale, but the principle is the same. Even the truly destitute and hungry in the world suffer more from unequal distribution and political gridlock than from the exaggerated idea that frivolity at one end of the world creates deprivation in another. Even though there are boundaries, more specifically ecological and environmental, frivolous consumption is not in itself a huge problem for the economy or society, and might in fact be a necessary condition of prosperity – which is, of course, exactly what Georges Bataille meant with his notion of the general economy.

If we examine what we as humans consume, necessities represent but a tiny sliver of our total consumption. Our clothes as far too fashionable and elegant to be understood as mere necessities; we eat food that is much more refined than is needed for survival; and basically all the culture and media we consume is a sheer waste if seen from a necessity perspective. Many think that this is positive proof that Western society is living in an unsustainable way, but I believe this is something of a misunderstanding. Instead, we might try to understand that our advanced economy is something more than an engine of survival, more than something that makes our often frivolous expenditures possible. If the human race had stuck to an economic model where only necessities for survival were allowed, humanity today would consist of maybe just 100,000 people, living mainly in warm coastal areas, hunting a little for food and spending the rest of their time in idle conversation (and sex).

But whereas some might see this as an idyllic and ideal state, this is not the world we live in. Instead, we live in an economy which thrives on expansion, creating ever more frivolities and a lot of good things besides. The development of the economy needs to be done in a reasoned manner, obviously, but to think that we could rid ourselves of our frivolousness is akin to wishing we could rid our world of billions of people and travel back to the Stone Age. Since at least the Bronze

Age humans have been busy creating and consuming the unnecessary – jewelry, ornaments, toys and bone combs. But at the same time we have developed a marvelous capacity for ignoring our love of consumer products, and what is even more amazing, developed the skill of being able to convince ourselves that all these things are necessities.

Phone Mania

Fast forward to now. Today, most of us feel that a mobile phone is a necessity. Managing without one seems really, really difficult. Our parents managed just fine without them, and as strange as it might seem, humanity did somehow get through several millennia without access to mobile phones, and another hundred years with only landlines to rely on. Despite this, today we find it increasingly difficult to imagine a world without the mobile phone, and as a result use words like "need" and "necessity" when talking about them. Our brain is here again up to its old tricks, but this time it's trying to make us think that our actions are much more serious and grown-up than they really are.

OK, but what has this got to do with creativity? More than you would think. The grown-up part of us tries to convince us into believing that our own behaviour can always be understood as the result of grown-up decision-making. Sadly, the same part also limits the way in which we generate new ideas. An excellent example of this comes from the innovation consultants' beloved concept of "needs". If you speak to business developers or creativity consultants tasked with helping businesses develop their ideas, one of the recurring things they say is that you need to identify unfulfilled needs among consumers, and then respond to this. This might sound sensible at first glance, but this is actually a really stupid idea.

Take, for instance, the Nintendo Wii, the massively successful gaming console. Before this product became known to me, I cannot recall having had a need for a games machine that you could control by waving a hand-control around. The thought of such a machine existed nowhere in my mind, and therefore I could hardly feel a need for it.

Now that I've seen one, I feel I absolutely need it, even that I must own one. So this is a need generated by the introduction of a new product.

It is in this way that creative product development is something quite different from discovering needs, and instead a question of dreaming up the unthinkable – something that could be turned into a need. If one accepts the typical framework that developing the new should be about a serious and grown-up hunt for the necessary and reasonable, you will never dream up a Wii, or a mobile phone, or the notion of an energy drink called Red Bull. All these are products by people who had the capacity to think outside the adult view of the world, people who could let go of the serious – dreamers with the playful thinking of children. And this is why they could create these fantastically successful ideas.

Reality, Shock and Awe

Adult conventions and the belief in the serious kill creativity not because there is something particularly non-creative in being an adult, but because of our innate tendency to apply the mature, rational thinking of everyday living to idea generation. The creation of novel ideas is something completely different, and requires that we can dream ourselves far beyond utilitarian rationalizations, explanations and talk about needs.

Adult conventions and the belief in the serious kill creativity not because there is something particularly non-creative in being an adult, but because of our innate tendency to apply the mature, rational thinking of everyday living to idea generation.

To really drive this home, consider the following. During one period, the bestselling program, or app, for the Apple iPhone was a product succinctly titled iFart. Yes, the number one product for one of the most hyped and admired technologies of our era had no use beyond being able to imitate the sound of human flatulence, albeit in an impressive number of ways. When the app was launched at the end of 2008, it saw more than 100,000 downloads in two weeks, giving the developer a quick payday. Now imagine the following scenario: this happy digital fartrepreneur is going to a business plan competition or stepping in front of an internal assessment committee to present his idea. "Yeah, well, I have this program that can… make fart sounds." Does anyone think that this idea would have been met with praise? Or that it could have won a competition? Of course not. The idea behind this product was stupid, silly and childish, and clearly nothing to invest in. There was just one problem. It worked like gangbusters. It just goes to show: nobody knows anything.

Want to become better at generating ideas? *Make yourself sillier.* Ignore what people "need", or what "works", or what people are "prepared to pay for". None of the models that have guided consumer behaviour in the past are guaranteed to work in the future, and every attempt to try to be rational when thinking about future business opportunities is condemned to be a prisoner of history. In fact, our rationality is always a product of our past, whereas creativity reaches towards the future.

Our rationality is always a product of our past, whereas creativity reaches towards the future.

When Apple introduced the iPod, a majority of commentators and business pundits declared it to be a bad idea, even a stillborn one. When the game *Guitar Hero* was launched, a lot of people laughed at the dinky plastic guitar and simplistic game-play. For many, many years, people have predicted the imminent decline and demise of the coffee shop chain, Starbucks. And, which I never tire of pointing out, when the Swedish entrepreneur Ingvar Kamprad started IKEA with the belief that people would be prepared to buy furniture in flat boxes and assemble it themselves, a lot of competitors laughed and ridiculed him.

But this is NOT similar to music executives turning down the Beatles or investors refusing to give early stage financing to Google – quite the contrary! In almost every one of the cases that the creativity literature incessantly repeats as examples of stupid choices, these have stood up as quite reasonable decisions within the context in which they were made. It was wholly rational to doubt Apple during their first stumbling steps, and to turn down the mop-tops from Liverpool. In fact, this might have been the only rational thing to do. The problem was that it was *the perfectly wrong time to be rational!*

The Off-Road of Reason

The rational and the creative are always in conflict with each other, and will always be so, as rationality is a question of acting in accordance with what we know and what our experience tells us, while creativity involves breaking with the framework of history and accepted knowledge. As "rationality" can be defined as the conditioned framework we use to handle specific situations, and as creativity could be defined as breaking with frameworks, the conflict between these two is something that is, logically, a necessity. This means that in order to become more creative you have to accept that certain things need to be left behind. More specifically, in order to become more creative you have to give up the belief that the process can be controlled or rationalized – you have to make yourself less rational and more silly.

> In order to become more creative you have to give up the belief that the process can be controlled or rationalized – you have to make yourself less rational and more silly.

Despite what some people think, this doesn't mean that creativity is synonymous with one of those dreadful brainstorming sessions where people simply throw out any old nonsense and where criticism is forbidden. This is, simply put, a cop-out. What a creative mindset demands is not a total lack of impulse control, but rather the capacity to reflect upon your mindset, your desire for rationality and control. This means being able to let go of preconceived notions of how things have worked before. What the conflict between the rational and the creative means is that you cannot stick to the belief that there is A Grand Plan, a secure path, an existing framework that you're supposed to fit your work to. The creative impulse is scary, because it means that we are navigating without a map, in a country that isn't even there yet. But this is also why it can be so exciting, and not only because it gives us a reason to tweak the noses of those who are still in love with an ordered approach.

> The creative impulse is scary, because it means that we are navigating without a map, in a country that isn't even there yet.

This also means that the process through which ideas are generated needs to be subjected to a certain amount of pressure and friction, and that just throwing up ideas simply isn't enough. The fact that you cannot rationally control the process through which the new and innovative is created sometimes makes people think that one is supposed to let everything just "hang loose", and that a structured approach is by definition a bad thing. In fact, it is just the other way around. Since we cannot know in advance which idea will in fact fly, which idea will prove to be a brilliant solution to a problem that no one knew they had, we must, in the process of creativity, learn how to catch hold of an idea rather than uncritically "[l]etting a hundred flowers blossom" (as Mao Zedong put it).

The amazing thing about kids is not their capacity for dreaming, or that they can generate weird notions, or that they are the original hedonists, but their capacity for believing. If a kid gets the idea that he or she is a pirate, no amount of rational argument or proof will change this fact. If a boy decides that he's a Martian, that's just how things *are,* and the bed *is* a spaceship. That this is irrational is beside the point. In the same way, creativity does not require that all ideas be given equal prominence, and the kid imagining he is on his way home to Mars doesn't think that his spaceship is a shark at the same time, as that would just be stupid.

Instead, the second key lesson here is that we need to be able to believe in our ideas, despite the many ways in which they can be picked apart. In this, criticism is a good thing, as it sharpens our ideas and steels us in our way forward. If you want to take a new idea forwards, rational justifications and uncritical praise are not enough. Such mollycoddling will not help us take a truly radical idea forward, and might in fact hinder us in the process. Kids are frivolous in their thinking, but can be ruthlessly critical at the same time. This, coupled with their capacity for believing in the new, is what makes them such perfect templates for the creative thinker. Learning from them is hard, but no one promised you it would be easy.

Kids are frivolous in their thinking, but can be ruthlessly critical at the same time. This, coupled with their capacity for believing in the new, is what makes them such perfect templates for the creative thinker.

IMPROPER QUESTIONS

Having come this far, a quick test might be in order. Most companies and organizations claim they want to be creative. But how can we check if they are? There is a simple test to measure this, here and now, in order to see just how creative your organization is or could be.

Start by answering the following questions:
• What can one never do?
• What is forbidden?
• What is inappropriate in our industry or company?

Then answer the following:
• When did I/we last do any of the above?
• Why did I/we not do any of the above?

PART III

Thus far, we've focused on challenging the secret box of our thinking, i.e., how we can reach the innate limitations and tendency for comfortable thinking that characterizes the human brain. Hopefully you've started to question your own thinking, and challenge your own version of this secret box. But this is not enough, not by far. Once we've started breaking with conventional, comfortable thinking, we need to start reassessing the context in which our thinking takes place. We have a number of taboos in our thinking, and the strange thing is that creativity can highlight so many of them. In the following section, we'll explore this realization. We'll reassess a number of assumptions that affect how organizations can handle dangerous thinking, and in addition we'll examine some things that are less dangerous than they might seem.

REASSESSING
THE CONTEXT

NURTURE YOUR ENEMIES

In order to have an enemy, one must be somebody. One must be a force before one can be resisted by another force. A malicious enemy is better than a clumsy friend.

—Anne Sophie Swetchine

It is an obvious and self-evident truth that the creative process needs aid and support to prosper. In fact, this is so self-evident that talking about it seems rather unnecessary, like the ritual utterances of CEOs at yearly meetings or politicians in election season.

Less self-evident, and therefore much more interesting, is that creativity needs opposition, and that when properly used, these enemies are worth their weight in gold.

Creativity needs opposition, and that when properly used, these enemies are worth their weight in gold.

A very special story is repeated over and over in books, speeches and people's experiences of creativity in organizations, and that is the story of "the others", the boring ones, the ones that just don't get it. I'm sure you've heard it before. Chances are you've told this story as well. In its standardized form it goes something like this: "We have a culture where one is suspicious of new ideas, and if I bring in something novel there is always someone who says that it's stupid or that we've already tried it and that it didn't work." After this story the convention is to sigh deeply to signal how idiotic these other, boring people are. If you're a lecturer or a consultant, you're then supposed to say something about how destructive "those people" are, and how they should be educated to be less negative. One might even add that they should be placed in re-education camps. OK, that's never said, but it's often heavily implied…

This is stupid. REALLY stupid. *Nay-sayers and critics are amazing, wonderful people,* and absolutely necessary for creativity and creative organizations. If an idea is supposed to have a chance, it needs to be subjected to resistance, for it is in such contentious surroundings that an idea can be tested and developed. If everyone nods and agrees, the issue simply hasn't been explored enough. At the very least, you can be sure that an idea that hasn't been pushed to the point where people start squirming uncomfortably in their chairs hasn't been through a rigorous enough testing. The nodding and humming that one so often hears in meetings (the ones we seem to want to have more of), are little more than comfortable responses, signals that people are accommodating ideas they are already familiar with. An idea that never runs into a nay-sayer or a person that does not agree must be a bad one, as it quite obviously doesn't provoke or challenge nearly enough. So take this phrase and memorize it: *If everyone agrees, it's a bad idea!*

To develop really great ideas, it is important to force them to the point where they create a sense of friction between themselves and the status quo. As the previously mentioned Joseph Schumpeter pointed

> **To develop really great ideas, it is important to force them to the point where they create a sense of friction between themselves and the status quo.**

out, the truly valuable ideas are those that create a significant change in the world, and these types of changes are never completely free from resistance, friction and destruction. Every productive idea will attack something existing, make some way of working obsolete, deprive somebody of their power base. This is not a bad thing in itself, as it is through such movements that our organizations and society can develop. But it means that every truly valuable idea will be accompanied by a true enemy, and that idea will be subjected to the accompanying creative destruction. It also means that we can gain a lot by taking a serious look at the enemies of an idea.

Kill Consensus Dead

The most dangerous idea ever introduced to the arena of decision-making is the notion of consensus. The belief that everyone is supposed to have the right to comment on, and even influence, every change in an organization does, as both the research and people's experiences show, lead to bland and watered-down solutions that neither provokes nor energizes anyone. Consensus thinking is the conceptual sibling of the belief that creativity can be a generally fun and nice thing, a comforting and comfortable process that doesn't antagonize anyone. Consensus is thus antithetical to real creativity and innovation.

The problem is that our business culture has become timid and spineless, focused on ensuring that no one gets offended and that everyone contributes – and thus not unlike modern kindergartens, if with less fun outings. In such an environment ideas will, by necessity, develop as pale and bloodless shadows of themselves. In such organizations, good ideas will die out not due to resistance, but its opposite – the numbing feeling that nobody really cares. We are culturally programmed to dislike criticism, and there are many organizations where criticism is delivered in a destructive and lazy manner. But the solution here is not to get rid of the critics, but to make them better and more useful.

WE NEED BETTER CRITICISM!

Productive Resistance

The concept of constructive criticism is often misunderstood: although people often ask for criticism, what they really mean is, "say nothing negative". All the while, people who dish out criticism hide behind the term, while all they really want is to be mean-spirited. However, the characteristics of constructive criticism are neither especially kind nor destructive. Instead, we might say that all criticism is constructive if it engages with an idea on its own terms. To say, "This won't work because we've tried it before", is a lazy approach that engages more with the history of an organization than the possibilities of a new idea. However, the comment: "Your idea builds on completely flawed assumptions, and I'll show you how", is constructive even though it might be devastating, as it engages with the idea on its own terms. People who are capable of delivering this second type of critique are exceptionally important for the creative organization, as they stand as guards against the dominance of pale and watered-down ideas. At the same time, they make it clear for those who want to enact something new what the rules of engagement are and what needs to be overcome to create a change.

> A key skill in leading a creative organization is the ability to create good conflicts, the kind that can take an organization to the next level.

This **productive resistance** is something that every good leader should try to embed in their organization, as it is such resistance that can sharpen the organization's thinking and ideation. As Saj-nicole Joni and Damon Beyer write in their *Harvard Business Review* article, "How to Pick a Good Fight", a key skill in leading a creative organization is the ability to create good conflicts, the kind that can take an organization to the next level. Part of this skill is the capacity to find and nurture enemies, while another is to create a culture where conflicts are not seen as destructive but productive. The good enemy of a creative idea is one who offers productive resistance, and who can lose a battle gracefully. A bad friend of creativity is one who doesn't challenge, and therefore is part of the wall of silence that kills far more ideas in organizations than criticism ever has.

> A bad friend of creativity is one who doesn't challenge, and therefore is part of the wall of silence that kills far more ideas in organizations than criticism ever has.

Enemies of this specific, productive kind are critically important for creatives, as they act as a form of friction in the organization, a resistant surface against which you can both test and hone an idea against. Superstar auto designer Jerry Hirshberg has called it "creative abrasion", but the terminology is not the important thing. The key thing for the leader is how to nurture good enemies, all in order to create the best environment for good ideas, and show the organization that being an outsider is also a useful function. Consensus reduces us all to the same grey mass, but serious creativity is all about confrontation and scandal.

Scandal!

Pay attention: if you want to be seriously creative, you should really be creating many more scandals. Consider Yves Saint Laurent, for instance. In 1966 he, as part of his *Pop Art* collection, introduced a suit for women, a strict tuxedo-like piece known as *Le Smoking*. It immediately created a scandal, with its androgynous lines and its improper idea about women being able to wear trousers as evening wear. A lot of people thought that the fashion designer had gone too far, and saw the suit as positive proof that fashion was a sick attack on society's values. Was this criticism damaging to YSL? On the contrary, it made it obvious both to him and others that there was something in *Le Smoking* which hit a nerve, something that challenged and opposed previous ideas about the proper and appropriate. Without this reaction, the suit would not have become the iconic piece it is, and YSL would have had a much harder time pushing through other unconventional ideas. The reaction was proof that he was on to something! What he learnt from this scandal would later be important when he launched his first male scent, which he marketed by creating adverts based on a nude photo of himself taken by the illustrious Jean Loup Sieff. The advert became another scandal, and several of the most important fashion magazines refused to run it. Naturally, the scent became an immediate and massive commercial success.

By consciously looking for points of friction in relation to his environment (not unlike the points of creative discomfort that exist internally in organizations) it became possible for YSL to get important information about what was truly creative in his work, and what was merely OK. My interpretation of his work is that he wasn't exploring scandals simply to become notorious, but in order to use media and his surroundings as a litmus test for his own creativity. We all become blind to the flaws and impact of our own work, and that which we think is important or creative in a project may well fall flat on its face when tested in the real world. YSL's strategy of attracting scandals showed in the clearest way possible which of his creations was successful, where he was at his most creative, and what, despite his intentions, was less than interesting. We can all use our enemies in the same way, as a sounding board for ideas, and this is why we should rejoice in quality opposition.

Three Important Enemies

However, for the leader who tries to make his or her organization more creative, this shouldn't be a question of drumming up more criticism, but rather about balancing the organization. What the leader must do is to create an environment where people both dare to present ideas, and where there is enough productive resistance to help these ideas develop and grow. The work in the former case involves motivating people and giving new ideas – even strange and improper ones – enough space to be fully tested. There are tons of books that discuss this. The latter issue is more complicated, and as it represents an aspect of creative work that isn't quite as pleasant and cuddly it is often forgotten, or just ignored.

There are three key roles within the field of productive resistance, three different types of testing and critique that an idea should undergo in order to develop. These roles do not correspond to personality types, and can very easily be enacted by a single person, but it is not uncommon for people to naturally fall into one of these types.

1. The first role is that of **the traditionalist** or **guardian,** the character that reacts to new ideas with scepticism. The importance of this role is not so much a question of what it can do to help an idea develop, but is necessary in order to gauge the idea. If the guardian doesn't start getting facial twitches and show an array of doubting looks, you might have to re-evaluate how interesting your idea is. In the same way as a barometer measures changes in air pressure, a guardian is your indicator of a new idea's potential, and a critical checkpoint. The traditionalist can also be a good test of whether the champion of

a new idea actually cares enough to want to convince the guardian. If the guardian becomes interested, the leader should see this as a signal. If the guardian gets pissed off, this might be an even more positive sign...

2. Once you've made sure that the traditionalists are well and duly vexed, it is important that ideas are subjected to a *devil's advocate,* a role which through sceptical analysis and rigorous testing, ensures that new things are not accepted uncritically. Being a good devil's advocate is a challenging job, which is why it is up to the leader of a creative organization to ensure that the few who can play this difficult role are taken care of. It is a role where you have to be able to question an idea from a number of different perspectives, but at the same time give the opposing party the space within which to develop and strengthen their thinking in a way that enables them to mount a counterattack.

   A good devil's advocate needs to be able to look objectively at their role, and not get unnecessarily emotional or personally involved. This is because the point of having this kind of testing role in an organization is less an issue of breaking down ideas and more about refining that which can be developed. If the devil's advocate gets too emotionally involved in this process, things can easily escalate into criticism for its own sake, which isn't productive for anyone. Instead, the devil's advocate needs to be able to lose with grace and even joy, happy to see good ideas thrive in the face of adverse criticism.

3. The last role is that of ***the competitor.*** Every change contains an element of competition, and in a creative organization there has to be ways to utilize the passion and the friction that competition can bring. If you look to some of the more iconic innovation projects you can observe how all of these had either a clear competitor or imagined one to develop in concert with. The energy this kind of challenge can bring should never be underestimated, and the role of the co-competitor is particularly important for creating better business ideas. This is essential, as it goes a long way towards showing that there is an impetus for development in the organization, and

that creativity is seen as something more than a hygiene factor put in place to make the workplace nicer. The challenge of a competitor might not be the best cheerleader, but ideas that have to be feted are very, very seldom the best ones.

All these roles are something that resourceful leaders will try to nurture in their own organizations, but they can also work on an individual level. If you study creative people you notice that they often, sometimes unconsciously, try to seek out people to play these roles. Creative people tend to have a competitive mindset (of sorts), and be capable of drawing energy out of criticism. They also tend to be their own worst critics, and often carry within them an internalized devil's advocate. Enemies, or maybe *frienemies*, are not in themselves bad things for creativity. On the contrary, we might, in all seriousness, ask whether creativity can prosper if it is loved to death?

COPY MORE! COPY BETTER!

Bad artists copy. Good artists steal.

—Pablo Picasso

Nothing is more symptomatic of how the discussion about creativity has diverged from its real creative possibilities than the way in which the copy has been treated within it. Or more precisely, the way in which the issue of imitation has been silenced and ignored. In the business literature and in various seminars, conferences and workshops, we are continuously bombarded with the message that originality and new ideas are good, while copied and old ideas are bad or unethical – criminal even. Such stupidity. Such complete and utter idiocy! If there is one thing that has hindered creativity in organizations and individuals, which has hamstrung the development of truly dynamic strategic management, it is our way of marginalizing copying.

> If there is one thing that has hindered creativity in organizations and individuals, which has hamstrung the development of truly dynamic strategic management, it is our way of marginalizing copying.

One way of summarizing this book so far would be the following: your brain wants to protect its secret box, the framework that generates norm(aliz)ed thinking, at any cost. To do this, your mind develops both a disguised form of traditionalist thinking, something which feels a little like creativity but is in fact a pale imitation of it, as well as a series of barriers that work to keep our thinking inside the secret box (without you really being aware of it). One of these defensive techniques is the way in which your brain identifies some phenomena as legitimate for discussions on creativity, while shutting other less suitable ideas out. Another is the romanticizing of certain aspects of creativity at the expense of others.

One of the most important aspects in this romanticizing is the lauding of originality. Almost every single book on creativity and innovation praises originality, new thought, unique insights. And these are, of course important things, worthy of praise. There is something in originality that we humans feel a very strong attraction to, and it is this desire for the novel that has enabled humankind to reach such dizzying heights. One needs to keep in mind, however, that this praising is both *a process of legitimization* and *a process of moralization.* Through our admiration we're saying that originality is not just something you can strive for, but something you *have to try for.* All the while, we're also saying that things that do not fit under the headings of creativity and originality are lesser, baser things. Simply put, this argument holds that originality is good and copying is bad; and we're all buying it.

Is Originality Such a Good Idea?

Reality isn't even close to being this simple and straightforward. It is not true that original ideas are always the best, or that copying is always inferior. This isn't true in strategy, it isn't true in innovation and it sure as hell isn't true in marketing. On the contrary, history is full of stories where original thinking failed completely, and copies managed to outdo originals. Take Google, for instance. A lot of people have praised Google as a truly creative organization (American business magazines fall over each other praising them for their originality, sometimes in quite sycophantic ways); and if you interview people you will find that a surprising number of them believe that the company created the very notion of search on the internet. Which isn't true. Google got in the game at a stage of massive expansion, and was at the time just one search engine among many others. Sure, they've always had a clean first webpage and a nice set of algorithms to run the searches, but claiming they were a true original is a bit of a stretch. In fact, if you look at

Google today, you'll see a company famous for its many brilliant web-based services, but also a company where the most used ones tend to be copies or developments of things invented elsewhere.

There is a distinct chance that you, my dear reader, read the passage above and inferred that I am criticizing Google. Nothing could be further from the truth. I do, however, understand how such a reading might be made. Since our culture has trained us to see every allusion to copying as negative, it is very easy to assume that saying that a company copied is the same as criticizing them. For me, here, it is the opposite. When I say that Google have copied *en masse,* I say it with praise and envy. *Google are brilliant because they are amazing copiers!* Nor are they unique in this. There are still those who believe that McDonald's was the first company to operate a hamburger chain. But they weren't, not by a long shot. The first fast food hamburger chain was White Castle, and there isn't much that is original in the story of how McDonald's took over the world – unless you count the story of the Big Mac, the burger that was developed against corporate principles by a minor franchisee (but that's another story, and a more dangerous one). No, what both McDonald's and Google (and many, many other companies) utilized was *the principle of n:th mover advantage.*

In strategic management we sometimes talk about "first-mover advantage", the benefits we see conveyed to the first actor in a new market. The problem, however, is that these benefits are often rather limited, and the associated costs can be enormous. The first company to enter a new business is forced to make all the mistakes on their own, to convince and educate the customers and to create and build the market. Companies that enter later might not be able to capitalize on the novelty of it all, but neither will they have to face the same uncertainties and costs the first mover is forced to carry. To enter as a sixth or seventh actor, as a late copy, can often mean that one can bring the best offering to market, one that has been thoroughly developed and tested – and to do so without having to pay for the associated development costs.

In this way, copying can be a highly successful strategy, even though it might not sound quite as elegant and alluring as being recognized as a great original. Still, if we look to the business world (and most of the public sector), the important thing shouldn't be how cool you look, but what kind of results you produce. The question is: how should we understand all this copying and learning within the context of creativity? Copying represent one of *the impossibilities of creativity*, a thing that doesn't sit comfortably in the modern discussion of creative development. Despite this, it is exceptionally important to understand the role of the copy in this context, for several reasons.

Strategic Copying

One reason is a different version of the logical paradoxes I discussed when talking about the problem of defining creativity. If we for a moment assumed that all the companies in the world that talk about creativity (which is, basically all of them) were honest and truthful when they say that they find it really important, wouldn't the company that completely ignored this be the most creative one of all? And when every company today is developing an innovation strategy, wouldn't it be the one that develops a *creative copying strategy* that would look like the most innovative of them all?

Creativity should be opening doors, not closing them. Creativity should – no, *has to* – be able to go beyond any given limitation and accept the possibilities that can be found on the other side of this. *So why not accept copying as a creative act?* Sure, it might sound incongruous, but there are many good ideas to be found in paradoxes. And since so much of what we're doing on this planet is a question of copying – all economic production, most of communication, and that whole sexual reproduction thing – it would seem quite odd if we couldn't find interesting and creative aspects in the world of the copy.

Nowhere is this more important than in the corporate world, since the processes of business are such that different aspects of copying will always be present and influential. The funny thing is, that even though business leaders often put a lot of resources into trying to copy the innovative strategies of other copies – and what is the genre of business literature if not attempts at copying "best practices" – there are very few corporations with explicit and thought-out strategies for copying. Once again, our tendency to moralize limits us from realizing our full potential.

All creativity has some form of copying at its very heart, even when the creative act involves both trying to combine and copy in order to introduce something new to the world. We often turn myopic in the face of this, and focus solely on the eureka-moment of an original discovery, but the fact is, if we got better at copying, the other aspects of creativity would work better as well. This is in fact a rerun (copy?) of the earlier example, where we contrasted the car engine's efficiency with the size of the gas tank. The problem is that our fundamentally lazy brain shudders and turns away when we try to think about how to copy more effectively. It feels wrong, possibly illegal, and at the very least doesn't sound like something serious people in respectable businesses get up to. Yet it is this very thing that many leading artist, designers and other creative types excel at.

If you study the work of designers, for example, you will notice how the very best are incredibly good at borrowing influences from the most unexpected places, and that it isn't necessarily any divine spark that enables them to create the new and the wonderful, but rather an acute sense of how to copy and combine in the most interesting ways possible. The very best within the field of design are brilliant and creative copiers. In much the same way, we can see how many of the leading business people in the world are incredibly good at picking up existing ideas or business models and utilizing these in interesting ways. Basically, all great technology companies act in the way Nokia's CEO, Anssi Vanjoki, describes: "If there is something good in the world then we copy it with pride." No lesser icon than Apple's Steve Jobs has said: "We have always been shameless about stealing great ideas." And still so few us truly dare to take this to heart!

7+1

Wanna improve your creativity? ***Copy more, copy better.*** Creativity is not a competition in originality, but a process that tries to find ways ahead or working solutions to problems. To focus blindly on originality might in fact make you *worse* at creativity, as it limits the number of ways you can take to develop new paths or solutions.

But how does one get better at copying? There are some "commandments" I'd like to share:

1. **Stop being ashamed.** Almost every single idea in the world is an amalgam of old material, so allow yourselves to experiment with the ideas of others.
2. **Study that which works.** Everything that works or sells or otherwise survives in society contains something that deserves respect and consideration, and should be taken seriously.
3. **Sometimes you just need to change contexts.** That service is important should be obvious. But it takes a creative mind to copy service into contexts where it's been absent.
4. **If it isn't enough to copy one thing, copy two, or even several.** Creativity is a question of combinations: that is, the art of copying things and putting them together in novel ways.
5. **Small changes can generate big effects.** *Dancing With the Stars* is a copy of *American Idol,* but with famous amateurs dancing. Whoever thought of that little variation is rich today.
6. **People like what they already know.** Why create things that work in ways that people do not know, do not understand and have to take courses to learn? Copy the approach, change the content.
7. **Learn from each copy.** You can become better at copying, if you reflect upon the process. Artists learn by copying the greats. So can you.
8. **Learn from each copy.** You can become better at copying, if you reflect upon the process. And good ideas are worth repeating (!).

I'm obviously not encouraging people to flout copyright law, and just as in any other activity, you need to ensure that you're behaving in a sensible and ethical way when copying. But our reaction to this tends to be exaggerated and overly cautions, and just like no one wants to be queer zero, we're all afraid of being seen as less than original. And managers are often amazingly adept at amplifying these fears.

When Innovation Turns Ridiculous

Some time ago, I worked with a corporation where the CEO loved innovation. As a consequence, he'd put both time and a great deal of money into making the organization a market leader, run by an innovative approach. Projects that lived up to this model were richly rewarded, and ones that didn't were treated like the proverbial red-headed stepchild. I visited the company, in order to talk about alternative approaches to innovation work, and lingered afterwards to talk to a department manager, who told me the following story:

"We have two projects running at the moment, two things we've put our time and resources into. One of these is a full-on bet on an internet strategy with mobile applications, and fulfills all the demands top management have for an innovative project. [The corporation in question had, I kid you not, a checklist for creativity.] The other is more or less a concept we copied from the competition and filled with our own content, a quick and dirty project we ran in stealth mode. The problem I have now is that I need to present everything we're doing to top management in three weeks. My department is making a nice profit, but… You see, the project that the CEO loves is losing tons of money, while the other is a runaway success – and I don't know if I dare tell the CEO!"

Copying can make creativity bloom, and the only thing that is stopping us from taking full advantage of this is our habit of seeing copying as something shameful. But there is no shame in copying. On the contrary, it is a necessity. Instead of turning away, we should make copying our friend, create copying cultures in our organizations, and see how this approach can generate both brilliant new ideas and an understanding for the reinvention of wheels. We have nothing to lose but our preconceived notions.

Copying can make creativity bloom, and the only thing that is stopping us from taking full advantage of this is our habit of seeing copying as something shameful. But there is no shame in copying. On the contrary, it is a necessity.

CREATIVE PEOPLE ARE A PAIN IN THE ASS

Creative people don't behave very well generally. If you're looking for examples of good relationships in show business, you're gonna be depressed real fast.

—Jim Carrey

One of the big myths about creativity, and a dangerous one at that, is the idea that it can automatically improve an organization, and that creative people are always good for an organization. Yes, sometimes this is true. But always? Not even close... In fact, it is mostly academics who assume that bosses enjoy having creative people working for them. The fact is that management, if we see this as a function rather than as individuals performing a role, doesn't naturally tolerate creativity in an organization. And, which might be surprising, this is natural and not some specific flaw in management. Sure, it is easy to criticize managers for not appreciating the advantages of creativity, but if we take a dispassionate view, creativity and good organization do not make comfortable bedfellows. We could even say that *the two are, by nature, in conflict,* and that this can never be fully resolved.

Why do we have organizations to begin with? Wouldn't it be better just to have improvised solutions, getting a project team together for each issue, collect resources directly for the matter in hand? Well, there are two reasons we don't do everything like that. Firstly, it would be amazingly expensive to do everything in this way (the fancy word for it is "transaction costs"). Secondly, and less obviously, it would be really stressful and confused to solve things in this manner. Instead, we have structures put in place to generate a sense of security and stability; and, in addition, managers that have been tested and found to use resources sensibly, offering "good enough" solutions. Stable, ordered, maybe not perfectly efficient, but close enough. These are conservative organizations, not because they want to be, but because they think they have to be.

On the other side we have creativity. A good thing, obviously: dynamic, spirited, full of vitality; but also prone to destruction and disorder. The defenders of creativity tend to say that this is natural and necessary for any kind of progress and development – and for any company that wants to survive in a changing world. They are right about that. But imagine an organization that is fully creative, at all times, without rest or pause. It would probably be a pretty tough organization to work in. You'd barely ever get anything done, as you'd be caught in a constant whirlwind of ideation, with little space for anything like contemplation or production.

The Other Face of Creativity

Three cheers for creative people and all that, but we just can't turn a blind eye to the darker sides of creativity. If one talks to leaders who work with creatives – for example, artists – these people are just as prone to talk about the problems of leading such organizations as lauding the benefits. Both history, research and in all likelihood your own experiences, stand as stark testament to the fact that creative people can be self-centered, have difficult temperaments, have problems in finishing projects and a number of other idiosyncrasies that make them difficult to work with. My favourite actor of all time, Klaus Kinski, was according to all who met him an exceptionally creative person. According to the same people he was also insanely difficult to work with, had no compunctions with berating people he felt were less creative and thus less worthy, and even threatened to kill his director when he felt like it. This doesn't mean that all creative people are unbalanced, for this would obviously be a lie. But they're not always easy to work with, or nice, or well-behaved – because creativity isn't*!*

When you hear CEOs say that they wish their organization was more creative, you have to ask yourself, whether they really mean it? Sure, they'd like more creativity, just not too much of it. Many in the creativity business see this as proof that the corporate world is wrong-headed and that their talk of creativity is insincere. But this stems from a fundamental misunderstanding of both business management and creativity. You see, *most CEOs know far more about creativity than creativity experts do.* They might not be able to wrap it up in fancy words, and are not that good at running fun little games with silly hats and what-not, but they are acutely aware that creativity has many different faces and generates many different effects.

Speakers who specialize in creativity tend to present it as if there were no problems with the approach, as if every new idea could be painlessly integrated into the business's processes, and as if there were no disturbances introduced when people in the organization start getting serious about creativity as a method of working. Leaders know that this isn't true, and they know that the speaker isn't really being honest. The CEO also knows that the speaker doesn't have to take any kind of responsibility for his or her words, that he or she can make all kinds of claims, and then be on their merry way to the next speaking gig. When talking from a stage, all the problems that creativity can cause can be brushed aside with a few vague references to the necessity for change.

If you're in charge of a business, however, you need to be able to deliver results and see to it that promises are kept. And you also know that things are never as easy as speakers would have you believe. Sure, inspiration is a good thing, and a little more creativity will be very welcome, but the CEO knows that *claiming that creativity will only bring benefits is a lie.* And he or she is right in thinking this.

Setting the Right Boundaries

Developing a more creative culture in a company isn't the really difficult thing. This isn't even all that tricky: allow failures; reward interesting projects for being interesting rather than for generating predictable results; see to it that people get different kinds of inputs and experiences; and allot enough free time so that the employees can generate new ideas. The difficulty lies in making this culture productive, in seeing to it that the organization doesn't just generate fun ideas but that they can realize and execute them.

> Just as copying appears as a challenge to creativity, and exists as something necessary in all forms of production, a company needs to be able to harness many kinds of energies – and creativity is just one of these.

The realization of an idea takes a completely different kind of competence (something we'll return to in one of the last chapters), and the leader doesn't have the luxury of being able to ignore this. To create a good working culture one needs to be able to balance on a knife's edge, by both introducing more creativity in order to keep the organization from becoming sluggish, rigid and dogmatic, while also keeping a reign on this to enable effective productivity. Just as copying appears as a challenge to creativity, and exists as something necessary in all forms of production, a company needs to be able to harness many kinds of energies – and creativity is just one of these.

Corporate Candy

All parents need at some point in their children's lives to teach them one specific thing. Most kids love candy, and sooner or later the smart kid will ask why they can't just stick to an all-candy diet. When I was a child, this issue was illustrated perfectly in a book where a kid got a magical machine that could make any kind of candy or dessert. The moral of the story was, of course, that the child grew tired of it all, and wanted meatballs instead, which the machine couldn't produce. So, those of us who have kids have, at some point or another, needed to explain that candy tastes good because you don't get it all the time. *Creativity is the candy of corporate life.* Tasty, yes. Something you can get an urge for? Definitely. Something that can be your staple? Absolutely not.

The kick of creativity comes from it being something different, an alternative to the everyday, a break with normality. In the same way as a drunken Christmas party can be an exciting break with the mundane life of the office, creativity can be energizing specifically by being something extraordinary – but also lose its special dynamic if one tries to turn it into something normal and mundane.

The project management researcher Connie Gersick became famous for her studies of project work, particularly her analysis of how some points in time in the development of a project create an energy and a sense of urgency. She illustrated that in the course of a project, the half-way point and the deadline were both times that got organizations highly focused, and were times of intense action.

Similarly, when you're precisely halfway through a project you tend to realize that things are for real and that you need to step up your game, and this can help the project to transform and realize its potential. All this is, of course, a good thing, just as it is a good thing for organizations to think about and reflect on their creativity. But it doesn't mean that you can introduce just any deadline and imagine it will help improve productivity! Deadlines, just like serious creativity, are powerful because they represent something that is apart from the everyday reality of the business. To try to harness this energy by creating yet more deadlines can have the opposite result, diminishing its effectiveness.

Surviving the Creative Organization

It is the same with really creative people. They are very good at kicking things off, exceptionally important for energizing the organization, but they are not something you need to have switched on at all times. The break with conventional thinking that creativity brings is, of course, productive, but creative types come with their own baggage, in the shape of disorder and destruction. Sometimes, this is exactly what the organization needs. At other times, it is something that the organization could really manage without.

The leading of creative people and the creative organization is thus a process where you need to balance two different leadership styles. On the one hand, you have to create the freedom and the security within which creativity can bloom. But the other function, the one where you need to break up the creative process in order to execute your ideas, this is often much more difficult. This is partly because organizations that are dominated by creativity quickly get used to a less forceful leadership, one existing mainly in the background. The main leadership problem lies in the difficulty of being able to get the organization to switch between phases of free creativity and phases where production and efficiency are prioritized, and to do so in a way that people feel comfortable with.

In the best of all possible worlds, an organization or a company would be filled with people that are all hard at work developing their thinking, while the organization has at the same time the capacity to switch between idea-time and go-time with no friction. Reality seldom works this well. We have a tendency to stick to one of these two tracks, and since organizations, by their very nature, are geared towards stability and order in a chaotic world, the tendency is for most to stick to the less creative track. This can be a problem, and something that the leader of an organization needs to work on. But just repeating the mantra "more creativity is always better" will not get you very far. A more honest way of looking at creativity in organizations accepts that there needs to be more mundane work, and that leaders need to take this into account. It is easy to talk about how great creativity is: *living with the creative organization is a lot harder.*

YOU ARE NOT THAT IMPORTANT

There are basically two types of people. People who accomplish things, and people who claim to have accomplished things. The first group is less crowded.

—Mark Twain

OK, I get it. You think you're important. I understand. I think I'm important, too. The trouble is we're both wrong. We're wrong in so far as we maintain that it is our own, individual and unique thinking that is important in the creative economy of today. Western society has for a long time been exceptionally occupied with the idea of the individual genius, the lone creator, as we are a culture who truly believe in the romantic ideal of the creative soul. For romantic thinkers and writers like Johann Wolfgang von Goethe, Lord Byron and Percy Bysshe Shelley, imagining creators as great individuals, driven by a fire within, was necessary for their world view. Over the years, professors and administrators have been more than happy to agree. Since we are creatures of culture and habit, this assumption has survived, and we're still very keen on believing that creativity can be found only among special individuals. Times, however, have changed in a way that makes this belief increasingly difficult to uphold, and possibly even damaging to creative activity.

Today, creativity is no longer solely the domain of that mythical figure, "the creative individual". Instead, we're living in an increasingly complex world where creativity can be born out of networks, in teams, over Twitter, from specialist groups, delivered wholesale from our clients, or born in the great, unwashed crowd. In the last 15 years, creativity has been seen by organizations as generating value collectively rather than through individual effort. In other words, we now look to how *creativity isn't born in one mind, but is developed between minds.*

This is not to deny that there can be such a thing as individual creativity, but rather emphasizes the point that most good ideas are created through different kinds of collaborations. If we look to history, there are, of course, numerous cases where an inventor or a creator has worked primarily as an individual, but the more common situation is that great leaps have been born out of collaborations or as linked chains of smaller developments. This also highlights that creative organizations aren't necessarily those that have the most creative individuals, but are those that contain groups of people who are good at combining their knowledge and talents into greater wholes.

Conflicts are Fun, Conflicts are Constructive

The consequence of this is that you cannot capture the full energy and potential of creativity if you only focus on how the individual functions. It also means that we can explore how breaks in frameworks can occur in creative frictions between people. We return here to the question of opposition and resistance. If there is a synergic effect when people with different viewpoints meet, how is this meeting productive?

Let's take an example. Imagine you're the leader of a project team with the task of developing better technologies for purifying water in developing countries. You have a number of experts in the group, each a leader in their own field, and in this you should have all the requisite knowledge needed to solve the problem. However, at the first meeting a huge argument breaks out between two of the experts, who disagree profoundly about the right way to go forward with the project. Is your reaction to this disagreement to: a) try to calm people down and get the conflict under control, or b) see what results from the argument?

We often start from the assumption that conflicts are something that need to be resolved, and that the role of the leader is to get people to play nice and support each other's ideas. But how productive is this mutual applause, and the accompanying implicit acceptance of all the different fixed ideas that the individuals carry with them? Isn't an argument where current ideas are seriously, even contentiously, challenged much better?

Dangerous Hiring

If we look to Jerry Hirshberg, the previously mentioned auto designer, he has taken this point to heart. In a profile of his leadership methods published in *Fast Company* magazine, he's quoted as emphasizing "creative abrasion" and working by way of "hiring in divergent pairs". Rather than trying to optimize the harmony of the organization, he consciously hires brilliant people with different perspectives, and rejoices in the arguments this creates. We might call this *dangerous hiring,* as it does away with the comfortable notion of the creative organization as a haven of peace and tranquility. By taking a stand for friction as a necessary and productive thing in the creative organization, Hirshberg has been able to make his design studio, NDI, into one of the powerhouses of creative thinking.

Throughout this book we have discussed the problem of overcoming the limitations we all have in our thinking – particularly when it comes to breaking with our brain's tendency of defending forms of thinking it sees as "natural" and legitimate. In doing so, we have focused on ways in which we can observe and work on such limitations in our own thinking. If we look to greater wholes, such as a group of individuals, the possibility of breaking each other's frameworks becomes more apparent – and it is obviously simpler to think outside somebody else's box (rather than one's own). This is why conflict isn't necessarily a big problem within a creative group, even though it falls on the leader to ensure that this doesn't escalate into something infected and pathological.

And this is why everyone who works with their creativity must sooner or later realize that part of this process involves accepting that others can question and challenge one's own thinking. In the earlier examples of the project group for water purification or Jerry Hirshberg's divergent pairs, this meant that the role of the leader was to ensure that people can bring in good ideas, while at the same time exploring how the group can transcend their individual thinking and subject each other to a *distributed criticism*. This refers to a criticism that shouldn't be seen as flowing from one individual to another, but which instead questions the collective and combined assumptions of the group and makes it possible for the group to play off each other. This approach should continuously surprise the group's thinking and not get bogged down in individual competencies. In such a situation it is up to the leader to ensure that the discussion remains open, so that the group can go beyond itself and start finding solutions that individuals on their own wouldn't have done.

This puts great demands on members of the team to accept that the group is more than the sum of its parts. This builds what Keith Sawyer has called *Group Genius* in his book of the same name, and this comes in many forms. Keith Sawyer has been adamant in promoting the idea that creativity is primarily developed in teams, and there is much to support this view. Still, while the creative team is a typical example of collaborative creativity, we can think of many interesting variations.

Lose Control

One of the main reasons why we focus so much on individual creativity is the conventional idea that the serious individual or company needs to control the creative process. This is, in all likelihood, the reason why the easiest way to enhance the creativity in any organization or company, namely to *listen more to the people you don't want to give over control to,* is practiced so infrequently. It is a common experience: you see something in a company that you think could be improved, made more efficient or radically changed, but can do very little about it. It is also raises a question: "Why are companies so bad at taking advice from the outside?" During recent years, corporations' desire to learn more from customers has been very pronounced – things such as open innovation, crowdsourcing and the ubiquitous influence of social media and networks have become popular buzzwords. Still, the feeling from people on both the inside and the outside of big business is that very little actually results from all this listening. You can legitimately wonder why.

The reason is quite simple, and connected to a recurrent theme in this book. Our brain's primary impulse is to protect its normal way of thinking and being, and it is not keen to let go of this control. When we talk about developing our processes, the brain's instinct is to take control and ensure that it isn't disturbed – "business as usual". On one level we might really think and believe that it would be an amazing idea if our clients offered suggestions on how to improve our working methods. In practice, we're all battling with our innate desire to control the process and consequently ignore suggestions that come from the outside. We don't do this because we think the ideas are bad, but because we subconsciously want to stay in control. On this subconscious level, accepting ideas from, for example, customers, is to accept that we're not as important as we'd like to believe, and this goes against very deeply imprinted cultural assumptions regarding the primacy of the creative individual.

Therefore, it isn't enough just to say that "open innovation is our way forward" or "we're going to let the customers develop our processes" and think that this will suffice. To develop an organization's creative potential takes a lot more: you have to dare to do something that goes against everything you've learnt about how to lead and run an organization – that is, *to lose control.* Opening up to the idea that creativity can come from the outside is to accept that we're no longer alone in the driver's seat, and that we, in order to make the company relevant in an increasingly connected and transparent world, have to accept that the company in itself is no longer as important as it once was.

This is something that a lot of CEOs find difficult to accept, for it takes a very different form of thinking to manage in a world where strategy is no longer an issue of building better and smarter controls.

Humility as a strategic process is something that is still in its fetal stage in the corporate world, but in the same way as individuals increasingly need to accept that job security isn't a given any longer, companies need to face a future where they will no longer control everything. Not even production, as companies will be forced to develop enabling and assisting functions in a society where processes of value production will be enacted *ad hoc*. Put differently, this is a future where more and more control will be moved outside of the institutional walls of the corporation. Humility in the face of this loss of control will be a strategic advantage.

this is a future where more and more control will be moved outside of the institutional walls of the corporation.

We Are Not Everything There Is

In this kind of situation it isn't at all obvious that the best way to develop the creativity of an organization is to make the individuals within it more comfortable with their own thinking. Instead, it might be smarter to work with how the members of the organization handle a diminishing control over the creative process. In the strange world we live in, sometimes *it might very well be that investing in the creativity of personnel could make the organization less creative!* This is not because investing in people is a bad thing, but because a lot of creativity courses and the like work on the wrong techniques, making participants even more convinced that they're in control, that they're supposed to be the be-all and end-all of new ideas. In a situation where the important thing should be to avoid getting caught up in the idea that individuals have to control creativity, such courses create the false notion that creativity is locked in individual brains, and even that the creative process can be harnessed by a series of exercises that can be replicated and executed on command.

Of course, this does not mean that organizations shouldn't invest in creativity, or that employees should not be encouraged to contribute their ideas. But if all this turns into the massaging of egos, you've seriously misunderstood what creativity is about. Sure, it is a nice thing if people get a kick out of working with their creativity, but in the bigger picture, this isn't the most important thing. In the best-case scenario, creativity is a way to make the world a better place, and this is a world where profits and personal feelings of pride and joy are nice bonuses, but not central in themselves.

Compare this to believing the message of the well-mannered creativity consultant, with his view that we can all be super-creative, and how this develops a feeling that it is we, the chosen few (who've gone to the relevant seminars), who are the ones that have the right to claim to be creative. In this scenario, you are creating a mindset where it is exceptionally difficult to accept that some ordinary customer thinks they could do better. "Did they even buy the book? How can we be sure that they did the right exercises, those that make you more creative and which felt so very empowering?"

If you truly believe in creativity, you have to believe that it will surprise you, and that it can come at you from any direction. If you believe this, you have to develop a little humility as a creative actor, and realize that yeah, you're not really as important as you'd like to think.

If you truly believe in creativity, you have to believe that it will surprise you, and that it can come at you from any direction.

THE DIVERSITY OF DIVERSITY

Diversity: the art of thinking independently together.

—Malcolm Forbes

What do you think of when you hear the words, "creative team"? If you're like most people, you imagine a mixed group of people with different competencies and different backgrounds, where one of the things that make the group extra creative is this diversity. There is something in the concept of diversity that makes us think that when this elusive thing **Nothing works all the time, everything works some of the time.** is present, there will be more ideas, better ideas, more perspectives and a more creative environment over all. Sometimes, things are exactly like this. Not always, though, and just as you should always remember that *nothing works all the time, everything works some of the time.*

One of the delightful perversities of how the literature on innovation and creativity has turned Apple into an icon is the way in which it has ignored the remarkably non-diverse nature of the company. On the contrary, we might say that Apple is an excellent example of the fact that one can become a leading innovative company while completely ignoring the traditional discourse on diversity. Not that there isn't some diversity in Apple's organization – there is – but this has never been their guiding principle.

Instead of being all too bothered about what people think, Apple has built an organization that often goes directly against the fashionable belief that more heterogeneity creates better organizations. We have already mentioned how the company largely builds on the almost totalitarian thinking of a single person, namely Steve Jobs – Leander Kahney's amusing book, *Inside Steve's Brain,* is an excellent and heretical discourse on leadership. In addition, much of the cutting edge work at Apple is done in teams and groups that are defined more by their commonalities than their diversity. The most important of these groups is the one that is led by the design god Jonathan Ive, a group which has created many of Apple's most iconic products. The group has been with Ive for over 10 years, and almost everyone has stayed with the group once they've been invited in. It is said that every team member is handpicked by Ive, and the group is defined by an extreme loyalty and a very distinct homogeneity. Rather than going for superficial diversity, Ive has focused on building a team that is so tightly knit that he personally has, at times, opted against receiving praise for the designs, referring to the fact that everything is a product of the group rather than the individual. For Apple, superficial diversity never seems to have mattered, and this might be a very good thing.

Now, this is not to say that companies should become less diverse. Nor is it an attack on the notion of diversity. Diversity is a very important thing, and deserves to be taken seriously.

The Many Faces of Diversity

What do we mean when we say, "diversity"? On the most basic level, diversity is a word we use for introducing a wide variety of people into an organization, rather than just picking people from the same background. Creating a diverse organization is often seen as the business of choosing people from different cultural backgrounds, having a wide range of ethnicities present in the everyday life of the organization. The mental image of diversity is often a pretty mundane one, where the photos in a company's annual report shows a wide range of smiling faces with markedly different visages. To this we have to add the desire to have a good balance of men and women in the organization, particularly when it comes to top management (something that most companies still struggle with).

The problem, however, is that other kinds of diversity, such as, for example, sexual preference, age or socio-economic background, are often considered a lot less (if they're discussed at all), since these are more difficult to fit into our conventional view of diversity. Some forms of diversity are just easier to imagine, and if you think too long and hard about it things just get confused and difficult.

So diversity often stands as a nice notion to rally around, something we all support in principle but really don't want to critically discuss. To make matters even more complicated, modern research encourages us to view this through *intersectionality*, i.e., the notion that one can't reduce diversity to labels that describe people through one of their characteristics. Take, for example, a gay Muslim man from India; which label has preference – gay, Muslim, man, or Indian? Should we see a new hire as "ethnic" (and thus equipped with "diversity credits") or as a Nigerian woman who follows her family's traditions... by getting a PhD? It should be obvious that we shouldn't reduce people by applying simple labels, thinking of them as being *either* a woman *or* Nigerian *or* an academic *or* a punk rocker, which leads to difficulties when talking about diversity. For if we no longer look to simple characteristics, what are the building blocks of diversity?

Just Engineers

This also raises another question: what sort of diversity will lead to more creativity? I used to teach in one of the top programs in industrial management in Europe (in Stockholm, to be precise). Picking from the students I taught there, I could construct a project team of astonishing diversity – a picture fit for the most discerning of textbooks. Without the slightest problem I could go through my old students and create a group with a balanced gender ratio, all continents and a wide range of ethnicities equally represented, hitting all major religions and most major language groups. I could mix in both straight and queer individuals, people coming from old money and nobility complemented with students from working-class families. To really hit the jackpot, I could also ensure that both 20-, 30-, 40- and 50-somethings were represented. Amazing!

Despite all this, I'm still not sure how creative the group would be. No matter how hard I worked on the mix, no matter how many of the diversity categories I hit, the group would still exhibit one characteristic that might defeat all my hard work. Even though the group would represent a fabulous photo opportunity, they would still be a gang of engineers from the Royal Institute of Technology in Stockholm.

What this means is that any discussion on diversity and creativity needs to start from the question: *What kind of diversity?* In some situations, particularly when organizations are growing, we need a lot of different kinds of diversity, but when we talk of specific problems and specific solutions, we need to approach the issue with a lot more precision. In some cases, it is exceptionally important to bring in people from many kinds of cultural backgrounds: for example, where one needs to make sure that a marketing campaign isn't culturally bound or Eurocentric. At other times it's more important to mix disciplinary backgrounds, to mix engineers with anthropologists and marketing students, such as when we're working on product development. These approaches shouldn't be seen as mutually exclusive, but it is important to note that when we talk of creativity we need to be specific about what we think diversity can do for the creative process. In other words, we need to introduce some diverse thinking into diversity-thinking, just as creativity-thinking is in dire need of some creativity. So...

Does Everyone Have To Be Creative?

The answer? *No.* Why would they have to? What a bizarre assumption?! A lot of things in this world can be managed perfectly well without adding too much creativity into the equation, and a lot of people have lived rich and fulfilling lives without ever bothering with creativity and creative thinking. At times, it even seems that creativity can be a problem for achieving the good life – particularly if creativity becomes a source of stress. I've met many, many people who say that they feel a great deal of anxiety when they're forced into creativity seminars and the like, simply because they are already content with their work and their thinking. To condemn such people simply because they're unwilling to live up to the often harsh demands of the ideology of creativity seems a strange and heartless thing to do.

Of course, we could argue that everyone can get something out of working more with their creativity, and there is a lot of research that points to a connection between well-being and creativity.* But this does not mean that we can use this insight to demand that people in organizations should live up to some specified level of creativity. This is partly because it would prove that making this demand shows the company doesn't understand creativity at all, but also because real diversity in a creative organization takes into account individuals who aren't creative in exactly the same way. Yes, in fact every creative organization needs people who represent the "non-creative" (whatever that is), if only in order to develop the kind of friction and productive resistance we've discussed earlier.

> Real diversity in a creative organization takes into account individuals who aren't creative in exactly the same way.

In an organization that is characterized by diversity there needs to be room for the people who don't want to be creative, the ones who like business as usual, the gals who dislike change and the guys who just want to do an honest day's work and collect a paycheck at the end of the month. The way in which many creativity "experts" argue that people who aren't into creativity should be "educated" makes me very uncomfortable, and sometimes I fear that they honestly want to forcibly convert everyone to their own one true faith. What diversity, in all its forms, should be about is accepting difference. This shouldn't be read as an argument against, for example, special quotas or affirmative action, as these can be seen as useful tools for organizations that have got stuck in an uncritical homogeneity. Instead, it is a way of saying that diversity cannot be reduced to a series of recipes or checklists, and must be seen as

---

* The research conducted by the Swedish psychologist Farida Rasulzada (http://www.farida.se/) being just one such instance.

a process and an ongoing discussion, one where even those who prefer not to identify themselves as creative have a voice.

What Kind of Difference Are You Going For?

In the same way as a creative act can only be understood by its application, the striving to enhance the dynamics and energies of an organization by introducing more diversity needs *to begin from the standpoint of what you want to diversify from.* In an all-white organization, competing with other all-white organizations, it is obvious that developing diversity will be both productive and generate value. Similarly, an organization consisting solely of engineers, working in an environment dominated by other engineer-type organizations, will be enriched by the introduction of designers and artists. But in the same way as a strategy derives its power and energy from being distinctly different from other strategies, it is important not to let diversity be a concept defined *a priori,* and instead see it as something that grows and develops in concert with the processes and environment of an organization.

This is why the example of homogeneity in Apple is useful, and this is also why a serious engagement with diversity needs to have the courage to think about forms of diversity that do not feel immediately comfortable. Just as in the more general case of creativity, diversity cannot be turned into a comforting concept, and must be allowed to exhibit a degree of natural conflict and friction. Serious work on diversity needs to take two principles into account, and see these as complementing each other. Diversity should represent both a reflective attitude towards what homogeneity means in your industry/environment and a way to meet that which exists outside of your secret box.

Diversity should represent both a reflective attitude towards what homogeneity means in your industry/environment and a way to meet that which exists outside of your secret box.

The homogeneous structure of Apple can then be understood in juxtaposition to the idea that creative teams are naturally and necessarily heterogeneous, although the risk that such a group will, in time, turn more and more dogmatic is always there. As a solution, this one sits uncomfortably with how the world normally understands diversity and creativity, and is thus creative by definition. At the same time, this is a solution that is highly comfortable with its own internal thinking, and will thus have to battle different kinds of creativity issues. Still, with the example of Apple it is obvious that one has found a way forward that has worked brilliantly so far, and thereby proven that sometimes, homogenous teams can be a very good thing. Nothing works all of the time, everything works some of the time.

This shouldn't be seen as an attack on the conventional applications of diversity work, but rather an exhortation not to assume that the relationship between this and creativity would be simple or straightforward. For the great majority of companies, the stark reality is that diversity, even though it isn't a silver bullet for creativity, still represents one of the simplest ways of enhancing their innovative capacity.

If we look to the top management and boards of most corporations, white men are still over-represented, usually to a ridiculous degree. Diversity here tends to mean that top management consists of *both* white, middle-aged men with a business degree *and* white, middle-aged men with a background in engineering. And, if one really gets wild and crazy, a few white, male, middle-aged lawyers. In such a situation, almost any move towards more diversity, no matter how generic, will have an impact. In such a situation, putting a black, gay woman on the board is an excellent way of challenging the secret box of the corporation. This, as anyone can see, is a strategic step towards differentiating the corporation from its competitors and thus automatically a creative act.

PART IV

We've now reached the really difficult bit. What makes dangerous thinking so difficult and so demanding is that it can never be fully explicated. It will always break with definitions, models, ways of trying to control it. So no book can do more than just tentatively give some direction, and then hope that the reader is prepared to take the next step. A book on dangerous thinking can never really be finished, as dangerous thinking never is. At one point, I considered stressing this in how I ended the book, so that it wouldn't get an ending but break in the middle of a sente...

OK, I'm kidding. The book will continue, but it would be fun to write a book that ends mid-sentence, with the last pages torn and tattered. Still, despite the ordered nature and intact covers of this book, dangerous thinking cannot be given a final, definite form. I cannot end by giving you a refined definition, so I've chosen to end by celebrating the heretics that do not merely think creatively, but live dangerously.

THINKING
DANGEROUSLY

CREATIVITY BY NUMBERS

Greatness, generally speaking, is an unusual quantity of a usual quality grafted upon a common man.

—William Allen White

What's better, one really good idea or 20 so-so ones? Is it better to work for a really long time to get to one great idea, or to work quickly and produce 30 ideas of varying and unknown quality? OK, the questions might be posed in such a way that the reader can guess which answer I'm fishing for. *Quantity is a quality in creativity!*

When I teach creativity and business ideation in a university setting, I sometimes have my students do an exercise they just *hate.* It is a tweaked version of a classic, namely the one where you ask people to present a long list of business ideas, many more than they would usually do. The point of the original exercise is to make sure you don't stop at your first idea, but instead think through several possibilities, so you might ask people to list 10 ideas rather than three.

My version is a little more advanced. The way I run it is that I start by entering the lecture hall as though I'm going to do a traditional 45 minute talk. Then, out of the blue, I tell my students that we're having a pop quiz. And not just any pop quiz, but one you have to complete to continue the class. There will be about 40 minutes left of class time, and during this time everyone is supposed to write down 20 business ideas, and leave their papers on my desk. I tell them that I'll walk out of the room for the remainder of the lecture, and the ones that haven't submitted 20 ideas before I'm back have failed the class and can rejoin next year. And then I walk out.

The fun part is when I come back, a minute or two before the deadline. At this point, the atmosphere in the room tends to be somewhat strained. I once came back to find an inconsolable Chinese student weeping hysterically in the front row, and had to spend quite a while calming her. When the deadline has passed I tend to have a substantial pile of crumpled papers covered with increasingly sloppy handwriting (usually some 80–90 per cent of students submit as instructed). At first, I have to calm down the room, for obviously I can't fail people just because they didn't manage to generate 20 business ideas in 40 minutes. After I've done this, I ask whether they understood the point of the exercise. Mostly, I'm answered with silence.

In Praise of Panicked Brains

The point becomes apparent when you start looking at the ideas, or more precisely their progression. If you randomly pick a paper from the aforementioned pile, a pattern quickly emerges in the distribution of ideas. The first five ideas tend to be pretty good, but conventional and a little on the obvious side. They are the kind of ideas that the brain can spit out without any real effort, a kind of snapshot of a brain just churning out matter. The next five ideas tend to be a little more vague, and feel a tad hesitant. You can see in them that the student is less self-assured, and is getting a little flustered. The following five (#10–15) start to look a little desperate – they're in trouble now. In all likelihood time is running out, and the brain has spent its entire stock reserve of ideas, the ones it always keeps in reserve. The brain is forced to search a lot further out than it would normally do, and can no longer rely on its usual tricks.

The last five ideas (#16–20) are the ones that interest me the most, for they can show us what the mind is capable of when it needs to let loose and stop protecting the secret box. Driven to its limits by a hard deadline, the brain switches to panic mode, a mode in which it subconsciously starts using its entire register of ideas. Now, if you look at the ideas that are generated at this stage, they're not all good. On the contrary, a lot of them are absurd. But they're often absurd in an interesting way, and among them you can, surprisingly, find very, very good ideas. It is here, in a free creativity that isn't tied down by notions of how to behave or how to appear legitimate, that ideas can go beyond their normal limitations, as the brain can no longer draw upon its old resources to maintain its habitual barriers and defences.

Deadline Fever

The same process occurs when people feel a sudden and unexplained sense of illumination when they work very close to a deadline, and why students sometimes find that an essay written in a few panicked hours gets a higher grade than a more carefully crafted piece. In all likelihood, you have experienced something similar – the brilliant idea that you got in a tight spot, the improvised solution that turned out to be a stroke of genius, or the feeling you get when you work on a project in the small hours and suddenly just start cranking out great stuff. All this stems from the fact that in order to be really efficient, the brain needs to be short-circuited and jolted at times. This is also why a stiff drink can be of great help in creativity work, no matter what people say against it.[*] In my example, it was the time constraint and the ludicrous amount of ideas demanded that shook up peoples thinking, but we can think of any number of methods.

Creativity cannot be kick-started without some preparatory work, since serious work on ideas demands that we break out of our normal ways of thinking. To think that you'll be able to become more creative just by running through a couple of easy exercises is to misjudge the resistance against novelty in our everyday thinking. This resistance isn't just something that exists in modern organizations, it is an innate part of our thinking, an aspect of the brain's structural makeup. As

---

* On the question of moderation: I started this book by pointing out that I'm not your mother. This still holds.

neuroscientist Gregory Berns demonstrates in his book, *Iconoclast,* the brain is hard-wired with a set of roadblocks to creativity, and neurological resistance cannot be overcome simply by running the usual brainstorm at the company retreat (which makes a lot of the work corporations invest in creativity development almost completely useless). Yes, I may be labouring the point, but the brain isn't fooled by these little warm-up exercises. In the same way as you can't learn French by repeating a few standard phrases once a year for an hour, you don't become more creative by having a nice chat about it every now and then.

Creativity is like fitness, and demands continuous exercise. Make your brain sweat and force it out of its comfort zone. One of the better books written on creativity is called *A Whack on the Side of the Head* by Roger von Oech (cool name, by the way). The only problem with this title is that it can dupe you into thinking that there is a specific whack on the head that would turn you "creative". There isn't. Your limiting and limited brain is a tough adversary, and amazingly adept at getting back to a lazy and non-creative state as soon as you stop challenging it. It doesn't need *a* whack, it needs many, and it needs to get them continuously – throughout your life.

As soon as you stop provoking your brain, it falls back into its old indolent state, no matter how hard you worked it earlier; many experienced athletes have found that the same goes for the body, and it isn't any different for your mind. So in order not to become the thinking persons' version of an obese ex-athlete, you need to regularly give your brain little jolts, surprise bursts of activity to keep it fit. There are two elements to keep in mind here (the equivalent of mixing long and short distances in a running regimen): firstly, the number of ideas matter (short bursts keeps the brain/body prepared for activity); and secondly, working with creativity needs to be continuous to keep it fresh (you need those regular long jogs). A good start is to do a little, often. So: why not try the world's shortest course in creativity?

The World's Shortest Course in Creativity

It's cheap, easy, and a lot of fun. The syllabus is as follows: every day, try to find a way to discover something new, some kind of knowledge or insight that you didn't have before, without limiting the area from which such insights can come. A friend of mine, who flies a lot, does this by buying one or two magazines he's never read before every time he is at an airport, and then spends the time on the airplane reading them thoroughly. In this way, he uses the otherwise dull time in the aircraft efficiently by getting insights into ways of acting and talking and being that he might not otherwise encounter.

Personally, I try to keep up a regimen where I get up in the morning and enter a random word or name into either Google or Wikipedia, and reading up on wherever that takes me. This morning, my habit took me to the world of diplomacy, namely the lives of Talleyrand and Duff Cooper – fascinating rakes, both. No, I have no idea how this will help me in the future, but I am absolutely sure that it won't hurt me, either. As an added bonus I got to enjoy Duff Cooper's clever phrase describing the perfect career, namely to enjoy "brilliant success without undue application".

The important thing in such a process is that you need to work consciously on gaining inputs from places you wouldn't normally look. I've trained myself to do this, and one of the benefits of having a restless mind is that I'm naturally geared towards such wide-range searching. In any given week I may well be engaged in watching Nollywood movies (Nigerian movies made with almost no budget), reading up on theology and following the rituals of hockey fans. I have, for purely academic reasons, studied a wide range of alternative sexual practices, if mostly on a theoretical level. At one point I was obsessed with the cultures surrounding the building and collecting of model trains, reading their magazines and following their feuds (!?!) in internet discussion forums. During recent weeks I've used Spotify to listen to as much hokum blues by female artists as possible, while also researching the techniques and business models of the perfume industry. Think of that what you will, but it's more exciting than when I had a thing for glassblowing (no disrespect to glassblowers).

This might all seem very random, or as positive proof that I suffer from some form of attention deficiency disorder, but it is the result of a conscious strategy. I do not know what the future holds, nor do I claim to be intelligent enough to know what kind of knowledge I might need in five years' time. So instead of getting into the self-defeating search for "correct" knowledge, a search I know will only prove foolish, I try to collect impulses and insights from as many areas of human endeavour as possible, without the pretence that we could say beforehand what constitutes valuable or useful knowledge. Creativity thrives when thrown curveballs, and to keep it alive we need to keep working it. Rigidity is a devious illness, and creeps up on you. A lot of people stretch to stay supple into old age, but few remember to take care of their thinking in the same manner.

Best Before Date

In addition, we have to remember that creativity has a shelf life, and a "best before" date. Society develops continuously, and that which was considered creative and scandalous in the 1980s seems silly and quaint today. There is no way of bottling creativity, so we must face up to the fact that any serious work with it needs to be continually evolving: one-off whirlwind efforts are great for cleaning out the closet, not for changing your thinking.

Sometimes, people make the mistake of believing that creativity is a young person's game, as one assumes that the love of change that characterizes the life of young people will translate into a greater potential for creativity. This is wrong. Sure, young people can be highly creative, and since they are more susceptible, they can achieve great things with their limited resources (it's all about efficiency). Looking beyond this, it is in fact the older generations that have a greater *potential* for creativity as they, due to their age, have seen more and experienced more, and thus have a bigger platform on which to develop their ideas. Young people can be conservative as well, and old people, if they are prepared to work, can easily outperform young people in the creativity game – which quite a number of artists, scientists and innovators have proven. Age is not a significant factor for creativity. But this is true only if one is prepared to take more than one "whack on the side of the head", and dislodge the rigid structures thinking so easily falls into. Younger brains have had less time to get into rigid habits, and thus have an advantage. But this advantage is smaller than you'd think, and can be overcome.

It is all about wanting it enough. The simple exercise with which I started this chapter is easy for you to copy and try out for yourself. You'll lack the sense of pressure and urgency that an examining professor or psychotic boss can introduce, but this is a question of self-control. You can teach your brain to push itself beyond its self-created barriers, and you can develop this into a routine to be repeated regularly, to stop your thinking settling into a rut. In this way you can keep your brain flexible and agile, against its will. Mind over (brain) matter.

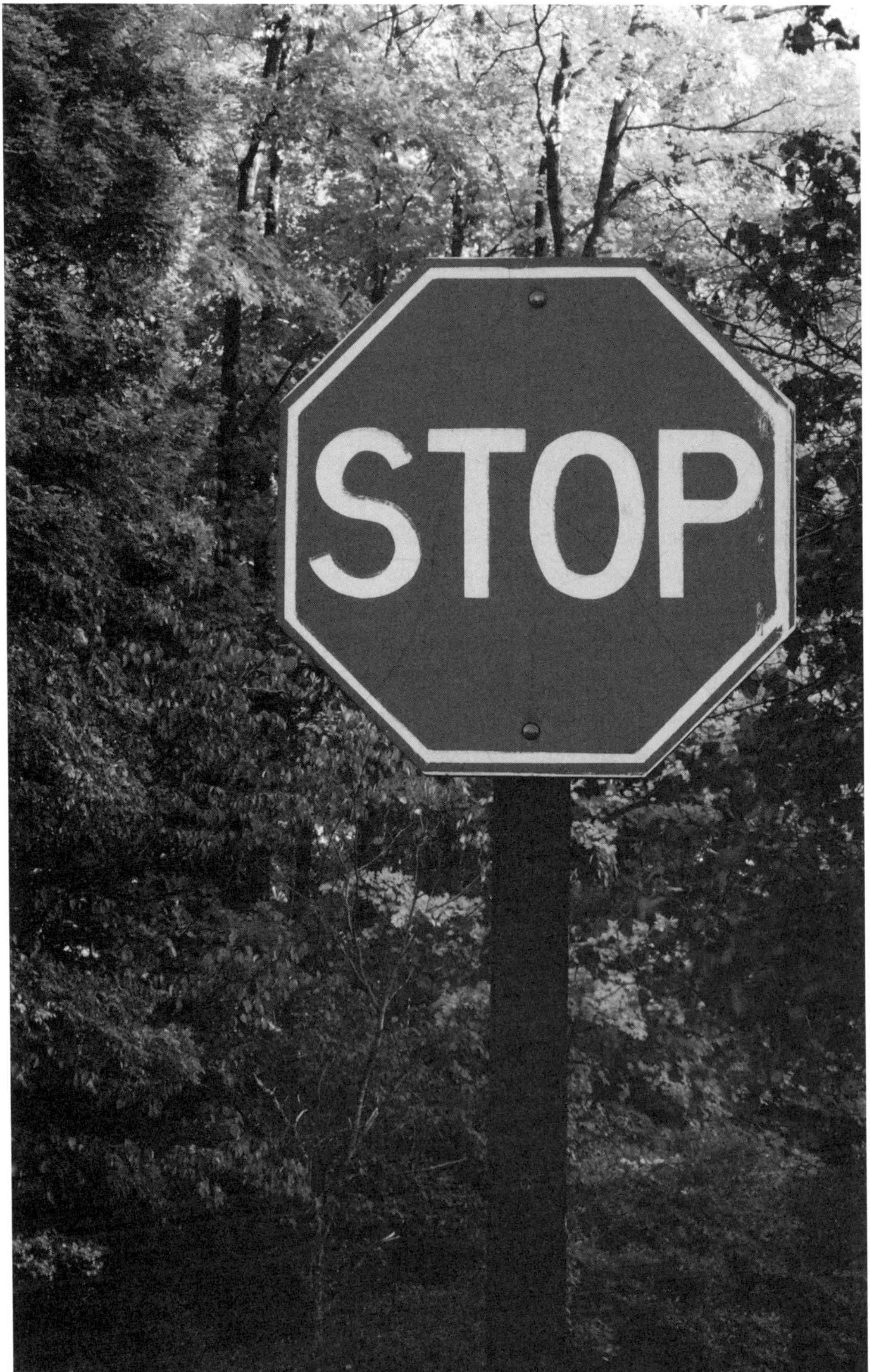
STOP

ACCEPT AND INNOVATE

Out beyond ideas of wrong doing and right doing, there is a field. I will meet you there.

—Jalal ad-Din Rumi

One of the many irritating things about people who're in the business of talking about creativity is their continuous insistence that you should always be questioning things. *Bullshit.* Questioning is all well and good, and often necessary, but sometimes creativity needs blind acceptance. If we're always just questioning, just treating creativity as permanent play, things just won't work. As, for example, Larry Bossidy and Ram Charan argue in their book, *Execution,* the capacity to act on all the lovely plans and ideas that mill around in the organization is what differentiates productive units from the ones that are merely showing potential. And people tend to forget that innovation work is both exhausting and time consuming.

Creativity and innovation are intimately connected, and we often assume that they can be treated as one and the same thing. But they're not. On the contrary, what's necessary for generating ideas and what's needed for turning these ideas into innovations can at times be in conflict, for where creativity needs freedom and space, innovation requires that you accept certain fundamentals blindly. This is not something that people often talk about, as it sounds so dreadful and dull, but it is true, nevertheless. Innovation isn't primarily about fantastic ideas, but about the hard work of realizing an idea, of making it come to life. Whereas creativity does not, and should not, let itself be constrained by whether ideas are productive, realizable or even sensible, something quite different is demanded of innovation – *accepting limitations.*

What's 2 + 2, Again?

Ludwig Wittgenstein is considered by many as the greatest philosopher of the last 100 years. One could write a lot about his thinking and its relationship with creativity, but there is one specific thing we'll focus on here. In his work, he happened to ask one of the most important questions regarding mathematics, and one that connects directly to the issue of rules and rule-following. Mathematics is one of the most structured systems of human thinking. It builds on rigorous logic, and is the basis of almost all those things we consider "rational". Our computers are mathematical machines, and maths is at the heart of the belief that one can rationally calculate what decisions need to be made in a corporation. Wouldn't it be wild if mathematics was built on some blindly accepted assumptions? Well, it is.

Wittgenstein asks the following question: "How do we know that 2 + 2 = 4?" Well, he says, we know because we've learnt the rules of addition. But he continues. How did we learn the rules of addition? Somebody showed us. But how did we learn the rule for rule-following? Well, somebody taught us that, too. We could go on, but the reader has probably picked up on the underlying issue. There is no final, rigorous foundation for rule-following, as one can continue to question the basis of each rule *ad infinitum.* At some point we simply need to accept that *this is how things are.* Without this acceptance no learning would be possible. If we look to how children learn maths, we see that most of this is in fact learning to accept the internal rules of mathematics. The teacher hammers home a series of points, rules and tables, and the important thing for the child is to have these drummed in. *And this is not a problem.* If we were to continue questioning things like the value of ϖ or how we arrived at the answer for 8 x 9, a lot of things would turn out to be impossible. Sometimes, we just need to accept the program, and sometimes questioning is pointless. The same goes for innovation work. Sometimes, it becomes necessary to accept that you're working on creating a better mp3 player and not, for example, building a telescope!

To take this daring step and say, "No, we're setting this in stone!" is often much more difficult for a leader than we imagine, and since it is so much easier just to let people sit in endless meetings and suggest things, many companies get stuck in an ongoing abstract process of change, where the need for more creativity is endlessly discussed but no one ever seems to get around to deciding anything. This is also why so many companies have so many meetings and lots of talk about change, but confusingly little strategic development.

As paradoxical as it sounds, sometimes, *a leader needs to be able to put a stop to ideation.* Not in a negative way, in a way that quashes future ideas and development, but in a way where the leader can say: "Let's ignore how things could be, and focus on how we can make something happen." This is, of course, more difficult that simply gathering inputs, or allowing one more brainstorming session, or having another creativity expert give a motivational speech, which is also why some managers shy away from this critical part of the creative process.

What Artists Know

Art is often presented as one of those things that we should take more seriously, particularly in the assumedly soulless environments of corporations. One often hears people talk about how lovely it would be if we could learn to work more like artists, who we assume are masters of creativity. Yet we rarely look at what we could learn from artists. Where creativity work, particularly in big corporations, involves much talking and playing around, your average artist is amazingly efficient at producing; that is, executing rather than talking about ideas.

Visit an artist in his or her workspace and you will not find a single memo or agenda for a meeting. It is also unlikely that you'll run into one of those artificial creativity exercises many companies seem so in love with. Instead you'll find prototypes, drafts and sketches, all crumpled

You don't recognize truly great entrepreneurs by the number of ideas they can generate, but by their capacity to realize a few of them.

up and thrown away, and more often than not a rather stressed-out artist that wishes you'd get the hell out of there, since she's got things to do. What is special about artists is that they realize that there is no point in talking things to death, and that all creation is about action. If you work in clay, you don't hold meetings to discuss the potential ways one could consider working with the clay; no, you start kneading, forming, shaping. Similarly, you don't recognize truly great entrepreneurs by the number of ideas they can generate, but by their capacity to realize a few of them. From this we can conclude that the belief that creativity is all about questioning is not only naive, it's dangerous.

One of the lessons I've learnt through my work with organizations is that in order to do my job well, I sometimes have to stop the organization from doing too much. At one point I stopped completely with creativity exercises, simply because I felt that they no longer had the intended effect. In a typical group, you'd have people who'd already done a series of similar courses or workshops, and who could therefore mechanically complete all the exercises. At the same time, some of the participants had never done anything similar before, and could thus be tricked into believing that they were making radical breakthroughs by learning the simplest exercises, the kind of thing any halfway competent consultant can run in their sleep. Put differently, the exercises no longer worked, and when they did, the effect was misleading.

But this was not my gravest concern. Instead, I'd began to realize that companies engaged in these things for the wrong reasons, and that they subconsciously wanted to do this rather than face the real challenges in the organization. So I stopped, and insisted that one needed to start from something much more fundamental: "Is there a reason for us to focus on creativity?" It shouldn't come as a surprise to know that the CEOs to whom I posed this question looked perplexed.

Even though creativity is a really great thing, it's not everything. One could easily be fooled into thinking it was, and companies tend to really enjoy discussions about creativity. But if focusing on creativity has become a way of ignoring other things, a way to feel that you're doing something while you are waiting for someone else to deal with the key issues, then it's become a millstone around the corporate neck. It's so easy to just look at the positive aspects, to happily shout, "Yes!" when the speaker asks if you "believe in creativity", that the thing can take on cult status. This is why it is important for companies that want to build a more creative culture to work with processes that support the realization of ideas, not just idea generation. And one of the names for such support is *leadership*.

> It is important for companies that want to build a more creative culture to work with processes that support the realization of ideas, not just idea generation.

To Lead is to Dare

The most important quality for any leader is courage. Decision making takes courage, particularly when we're talking about unpleasant decisions. Drawing a line takes courage, as does putting your foot down. Managers have to do a ton of things that are tough and less than pleasant. In light of this, it should not be surprising that many managers treat creativity as a nice break from all the unpleasant tasks, something you can do that won't make conflicts and which is seen as nice and fun by everyone. Creativity work can be a trivial diversion, so it is understandable why a manager might be tempted to go for it.

If a manager wants to be a leader, this lazy approach will not do. The difference between a manager and a leader is that the latter dares to take that extra step, won't let the organization treat creativity as a dead end of rumination and chit-chat, and demands action. This is also why it is one of the tasks of the leader to take creativity seriously, even in its less pleasant and immediately attractive forms. As already stated, creative ideas are not always pleasant for organizations, and can in fact generate feelings of fear and disgust. This means that organizations need leaders who are capable of allowing unpleasant (and therefore potentially transformative) ideas to be explored. Strong leaders can be identified by their capacity to enact changes that the organization responds to negatively. Strong leaders, such as Jack Welsh and Richard Branson (or, for that matter, Ingvar Kamprad), are not characterized by their capacity to get people to cheer for them, but by the way in which they can realize ideas that might otherwise become bogged down in the organization through fear, doubt or resistance. Richard Branson is particularly eloquent here: "Screw it, let's do it."

This last point – **just do it** – is the difference between companies that claim that they are creative and companies that really are. With a little practice, anyone can generate three or four decent ideas a day. Not everyone can take this to the next level, the one where you're not just ideating but acting upon this. An organization without creative leadership, one with a manager that treats creativity as just another way of keeping people content, will in all likelihood generate a lot of ideas, notions and possibilities. But is the company being creative? No, not really. As brutal as it may sound, real creativity demands

> **Real creativity demands that someone – and it could be you – decides to not just play with ideas, but to do something.**

that someone – and it could be you – decides to *not just play with ideas, but to do something*. Three cheers for creativity, but the future is not built by cheers. It is built by people who act, by those who dare to transform ideas into action.

LONG LIVE THE HERETICS!

Heresy is another word for freedom of thought.

—Robert Heinlein

The question is not whether we will be extremists, but what kind of extremists we will be... The nation and the world are in dire need of creative extremists.

—Martin Luther King, Jr.

It would be both intellectually dishonest and highly improper (in a bad way, this time around) to end this book in any other way than by asking whether the entire project has been a sham and all wrong. Why should this book be special, why should this book be free from the usual contradictions, wallowing in its own self-assuredness and complacency?

I can honestly state that I don't know everything about creativity. I've read tons of books about the theory, I've written my fair share about it, I've taught it in universities, and I've worked closely on creativity issues with many different corporations. Some might even say that I know a little something about it. But I don't know everything, not by a long shot, and I'm OK with that. I'm not even that concerned whether I'm right in everything I say about creativity, as I don't see it as my business to dispense eternal truths – something I like to leave to the priests.* I

---

* By an odd coincidence I am, however, ordained as *Reverend* Alf Rehn by a free church in the United States, and can even marry people in some states, but that's another story…

don't want to assert eternal truths, I want to raise questions, even about the process of raising questions.

The world needs heretics, people who are not comfortable with the *status quo.* You might have been fooled into believing that heretics died out after the church (and particularly the Catholic Church) lost its role as the guardian of eternal truth. No, the fact is, we need heretics today more than ever, now that there are far more churches and orthodoxies today to challenge with heretical thinking.

Today, we are asked to accept a whole series of things about the market economy as gospel, everyone is supposed to accept that "creativity" and "innovation" are self-evidently good things, and we are asked to be continuously in a process of change, as if change has been postulated as a law of nature. To question innovation or change doesn't make people mad, it confuses them, because the old truths have become both more widely dispersed and more embedded into the general ideology of society. The need for modern heretics is great, not only because heretics are agents of progress, but also because we have fooled ourselves into believing that we live in much more critical times than we do.

Heretical Leaders

At the same time, these are excellent times for heretics. During the Middle Ages, a mild form of punishment for lesser forms of heresy could be lengthy prison terms or banishment. More full-blown questioning of dogma could quickly lead to torture and death. Today, the authorities tend to be a little more tolerant. When I visit corporations and events, raising questions about notions of creativity and innovation, the very worst reception has been one of confusion and scepticism. Even then, the response has always been gracious. One of the unintended consequences of contemporary society's almost religious interest in innovation is that it has become much more accepted to challenge things, even ideas about creativity. And if nothing else, it has become possible to engage in a little *creativity aikido,* to turn its articles of faith against it.

It is therefore my absolute conviction that the world needs far more heretics, people who will not accept things as they are, champions who are prepared to cast doubt on the legitimacy of the current state of play. There are so many things that are presented as certainties and finalities, that companies will soon be forced to appoint professional heretics — *Chief Heretical Officers* – if they are to stay in business. Just think of the list of things that today are seen as self-evident truths for businesses:

- Branding
- Globalization
- Corporate Social Responsibility
- Entrepreneurship and Intrapreneurship
- Networks
- Green Management
- Growth
- Change Management
- Knowledge Management
- Sustainability
- Supply Chain Management
- Social Entrepreneurship
- Management Innovation
  And so on…

Each and every one of these "truths" need their own heretics, people who are prepared to attack that which we hold as certain, true and obvious. This is not to sabotage things, but because all forms of development rests on being able to sacrifice something, being prepared to take a few hits along the way, and seeing the old systems being partially dismantled. There is no economy without destruction, and the belief that one could have true and immutable truths for economics only shows that one doesn't understand the process of creative development.

Heretics are not important because they are closer to the truth than their more conventional detractors, but because they can challenge a system that has become too dogmatic. They can, in short, introduce the kind of uncertainty that is at the heart of all forms of value creation.

Try to control the uncertainties of this world, and you know you're wrong. Jonas Ridderstråle, one of the world's leading management gurus, has expressed this by stating: "Try to control the uncertainties of this world, and you'll go nuts." I want to take this much further. My motto? *Try to control the uncertainties of this world, and you know you're wrong.* It's not that we don't have the mental capacity to handle the uncertainties, it's the fact that certainties do not exist.

Not even certainties about creativity. My motivation for writing this book came from the horror I felt regarding how the concept I so loved had become domesticated and made proper, and thereby died a little. If one looks to history and great Medieval heretics, such as Girolamo Savonarola (1452-1498) and Fra Dolcino (1250-1307), the thing that characterizes them is not their scepticism, but how much they had faith. Rather than accepting a simplified and bastardized version of what they believed in, they were prepared to die for the truly radical nature of their faith. And I feel something similar for creativity, even though I am a much, much weaker man than they were – and thus not prepared to become a martyr for my beliefs.

Putting this aside, I feel quite strongly that the radical potential of creativity has been neglected because an army of consultants and motivational speakers have changed it into a series of cheap tricks and smokescreens. This is why I want to raise my voice and talk for a creativity that is much more radical than just a way to "have ideas and, like, think freer".

Can We Unlearn Our Good Manners?

Creativity isn't all fun, isn't all nice, and isn't something you should uncritically accept and adopt. If it were such a thing it would be far less powerful than it is, a rather harmless diversion. The same goes for heretics. It is normal to react negatively towards heretics, just as it is normal to react with a degree of discomfort to the true face of creativity. Real creativity isn't harmless and sweet, but a force that makes us see ourselves and our thinking as limited and incomplete. This isn't nice, or friendly or all snuggly, for real change never can be. So *I perfectly understand why one might feel uncomfortable with real creativity.*

Still, in this fear there is a serious threat. By seeing creativity and innovators as something you can domesticate into something like the corporation's pet, you're not only castrating your own potential for creating something new, you're sabotaging the heretics around you. A good friend of mine, an innovative CEO by the name of Claudia Suraga, remarked as we discussed this book that it would be interesting to get lessons in innovation from the people who never get a voice in such discussions – the criminals, the insane, those with alternative sexuality, priests and so on. Even though this book probably won't live up to her expectations, she immediately understood its point. This is because she is the very image of a modern heretic, a person who's not even prepared to accept everything unquestioningly. In earlier times, she would, in all likelihood, have been committed to an asylum or burnt at the stake.

The question, dear reader, is do you have people like Claudia in your network? What makes her a particularly good friend is the fact that she's never prepared to blindly accept the things I say, or accept that what I've written is the best I can do. She is a heretic's heretic, a version of the demon every creator has on their shoulder and who whispers *memento mori,* "remember you shall die". *Questioning is easy, taking it seriously is hard.*

For you, readers, the tricky but important challenge is taking what I've written seriously while at the same time being able to ignore it when necessary. Creativity is paradoxical, an energy that can never be fully explained or captured, and perpetually radical in that it always needs to break its own boundaries. If there is one thing I wish you would take away from my book, it is this: if creativity is all about breaking with how we normally see things, wouldn't it follow that it is also about breaking with how we normally view creativity? Heretical creativity isn't something finished, something set in stone, something defined. Instead, it is a clarion call, an

> If creativity is all about breaking with how we normally see things, wouldn't it follow that it is also about breaking with how we normally view creativity?

aber, the joy of realizing you've been wrong all along. Creativity is that which won't let itself be described or tied down, the passion and the desire, the striving to go beyond what you think can be done.

Burn 'em! Burn 'em Good!

At the very moment I write these words there is a children's TV show playing in the background. In this show, a panelist asks, how come a number of things that are acceptable for boys – smelling of sweat, having body hair, farting and telling dirty stories – are unacceptable for girls? My immediate thought is that this is the sound of creativity shrinking and dying, the moment at which we legitimize specific notions as unacceptable. And it is here that true change can be enacted. The first companies that accepted female sexuality, something previously seen as unmentionable, made a fortune. The same is true for those entertainers that dared to push the boundaries of what constitutes suitable entertainment. And all those fabulous heretics that dared to challenge the biggest institutions of their times have changed the world in ways that we can dimly grasp.

So keep cursing in church (any church), and keep your heresies alive. Don't stop being uncomfortable, for the world needs resistance, and all change has to hurt a little. As previously stated, it is by exploring the points of discomfort that you can find the potential for change. When the Catholic Church was at its strongest, heresy was a crime that you could be burned alive for. There is something grand, something amazing about this. The world's largest, most powerful and most wealthy organization felt that free thinkers were so dangerous that it wasn't enough to kill them; you needed to annihilate them so that other potential heretics would be frightened off from even trying to do the same. What a truly glorious image of the unfettered power of the human mind!

At the same time this poses an interesting question for our modern times and our future. How often do we run into this level of resistance any longer?* How often do organizations *really* oppose new ideas and

---

* To those that thought of it: yes, I'm aware of the connections that one could draw to radical Islam in contemporary society. This is an interesting issue, but not one I'll get into here.

heretical employees? When people in corporations say that new kinds of thinking does not get enough support, they don't mean that ideas are met with aggravation and chagrin, they mean that things get stuck in the mire of yawns, shrugged shoulders and general indifference. So let's turn the issue on its head. Maybe it's not the company that's boring and traditional, maybe the ideas are? No one gets angry, no one gets wild-eyed, no one wants to burn you at a stake... The ideas of heretics and revolutionaries were radical: we can recognize this from the overwhelming force that was used to beat them down, not from the fact that some committee gave them "support".

The same goes for creativity more generally. The heretics condemned by the Catholic Church, such as my hero Savonarola, weren't interested in being tolerated, they were interested in changing the world. They *knew* this would be seen as something dangerous, and were still prepared to fight and die for their views. The modern world has become a time of caution and playing it safe, and the bizarre thing is that the debate about creativity has accepted this and prostrated itself before this conservative impulse. So we talk about tolerance, we insist on support and understanding, and we present creativity as something recognized in a universal form. Real heretics spit on such ideas. What we need now are people who can shake the foundations of the corporate structures in much the same way as the earlier heretics shook the church – through direct engagement and not caring a whit about fitting in.

> What we need now are people who can shake the foundations of the corporate structures in much the same way as the earlier heretics shook the church – through direct engagement and not caring a whit about fitting in.

So long live the heretics, the misfits, the immodest ones, the dirty-filthy-nasty ones. Long live the childish, the indecent and the offensive. Long live all those who cannot be allowed into the drawing rooms of polite society! Right now, somewhere out there, someone who you, in all likelihood, wouldn't like all that much, sits and ponders things you would find unpleasant or stupid. Right now, there isn't a single person on earth that is more important to you, your company and what you do. For here is where you can find the ***truly dangerous ideas.***

ABOUT THE AUTHOR

Alf Rehn is Chair of Management and Organization at Åbo Akademi University (Finland) and formerly Professor of Innovation and Entrepreneurship at the Royal Institute of Technology (Sweden). His research has dealt with subjects as varied as creativity, haute cuisine, project management, popular culture, philosophy, boredom, innovation, and luxury, and has been published in both a series of books and a large number of articles. He is in addition to this a popular public speaker and a consultant in the areas of creativity, innovation, strategy and consumer behaviour, and has worked with top management in a wide array of corporations and other organizations. He is a devoted fan of Ethel Merman and the divine Patsy Cline. For more information visit his website at www.alfrehn.com